elegant Lettering
FOR YOUR HOME

REBECCA BAER, CDA

NORTH LIGHT BOOKS
CINCINNATI, OHIO
www.artistsnetwork.com

DEDICATION

For Dad and Mom, who encouraged my artistic endeavors from the start.

Other fine North Light Books are available from your local bookstore, art supply store or direct from the publisher.

METRIC CONVERSION CHART

TO CONVERT	TO	MULTIPLY BY
Inches	Centimeters	2.54
Centimeters	Inches	0.4
Feet	Centimeters	30.5
Centimeters	Feet	0.03
Yards	Meters	0.9
Meters	Yards	1.1
Sq. Inches	Sq. Centimeters	6.45
Sq. Centimeters	Sq. Inches	0.16
Sq. Feet	Sq. Meters	0.09
Sq. Meters	Sq. Feet	10.8
Sq. Yards	Sq. Meters	0.8
Sq. Meters	Sq. Yards	1.2
Pounds	Kilograms	0.45
Kilograms	Pounds	2.2
Ounces	Grams	28.4
Grams	Ounces	0.035

09 08 07 06 05   5 4 3 2 1

Library of Congress Cataloging-in-Publication Data
Baer, Rebecca
 Elegant lettering for your home / Rebecca Baer.
  p. cm.
 Includes index.
 ISBN 1-58180-578-0 (pbk. : alk. paper)
 1. Stencil work. 2. Lettering. I. Title.

TT270.B34 2005
745.7'3--dc22   2004050127

EDITOR: Holly Davis
PRODUCTION COORDINATOR: Kristen Heller
DESIGNER: Brian Roeth
INTERIOR LAYOUT ARTIST: Donna Cozatchy
PHOTOGRAPHER: Christine Polomsky

fw
F+W PUBLICATIONS, INC.

ABOUT THE AUTHOR

Rebecca's professional background as a technical illustrator taught her the importance of detail, which is evident in the graceful lines of her designs as well as in the in-depth, step-by-step instruction provided in each pattern packet and book she creates. Additional design experience was obtained while employed by a pipe organ manufacturer, where she created architectural renderings of organ facades. This aided in developing her creativity and polishing her skills. She entered the field of decorative painting in the early 1990s and earned the level of Certified Decorative Artist from the Society of Decorative Painters (SDP) in 1996. She has passed the strokework portion of the Society's Master Decorative Artist program.

A popular designer and instructor, Rebecca maintains an active seminar schedule both internationally and at home. She also participates in various regional and national conventions and is a participant in the Artists of the World Exhibition, a decorative painting exhibit in Tokyo, Nagoya and Osaka, Japan which attracts over 30,000 visitors.

Rebecca has developed the unique line, Simply Elegant Stencils, featuring detailed backgrounds and a variety of motifs that allow even the novice painter to create exquisite embellishments with ease. The stencils can be used for decorative painting and home décor, and are perfect for developing custom pages in heirloom scrapbooks when used with acid-free paints, chalks or stamping inks.

Rebecca is regularly published in the leading U.S. decorative painting magazines and is also a featured artist in Japanese publications. She has produced an extensive line of pattern packets and is the author of the book *Painting Gilded Florals and Fruits.* This book not only covers a broad range of techniques for those desiring to expand their creative horizons, but also offers attractive projects for those who simply desire a beautiful painted item.

Rebecca's stencils, pattern packets and books are marketed internationally through her Web site, as well as in retail shops. You can find more of Rebecca's work at www.rebeccabaer.com.

ACKNOWLEDGMENTS

Recognition must go first to my husband, Bobby, who is also the other half of my business, and to our two daughters, Jessi and Amy, who endure my creative preoccupation.

Special thanks go to my friend and cohort, Kathryn Fowler, for endless hours helping me with everything I do; to Debbie Culler for her expertise in assisting with many of the project introductions and for being available for feedback whenever I need it; and to my many painting friends, too numerous to mention, who continue to inspire me with their enthusiasm.

Many thanks to my publishing team—Kathy Kipp, who invited me to write this book; my editor, Holly Davis; and my photographer, Christine Polomsky—for making my photo shoot at North Light both fun and productive. And my thanks to the many people behind the scenes at North Light Books with whom I may have never crossed paths, but who have helped to make this book possible.

I also wish to thank the many suppliers listed throughout this book for graciously providing materials and surfaces.

Most important, I am grateful that God has blessed me with talent and that everything I design is inspired "From the Hands of the Creator."

TABLE OF CONTENTS

INTRODUCTION

Elegant Lettering for Your Home is more than simply a how-to book for completing attractive projects. Layout techniques and tips are also presented, providing the tools you need to customize designs as desired. Whether you prefer an inspirational quote or a favorite scripture to adorn your walls and garden gate, *Elegant Lettering for Your Home* illustrates how to enhance a variety of surfaces to create a welcoming atmosphere.

Lettering need not be elaborate to be beautiful. It can stand alone with understated charm and be used to create interest in otherwise austere areas, as shown on the first project, found on pages 22-27, which features etched lettering on glass. Combined with other decorative elements, lettering can become the focal point of a broader design. Two examples of this treatment can be found in project seven, the garden slate, on pages 66-73, and project ten, the magazine box, on pages 98-107. A third way to use lettering is as a separate but equal design element. On the recipe box, project nine, on pages 86-97, lettering is used to balance and enhance the eggs and antique eggbeater composition located at the opposite end of the design.

The variety of projects found within this book covers a wide range of applications—from home accessories to furniture accents to wall décor—and many can be completed rather quickly. There's something for every room in the house, not to mention the garden. In addition, you'll find suggestions for adapting these and other designs, enabling you to personalize projects to suit your own or a client's taste. The possibilities are endless. Use each palette as presented or vary the colors as desired to harmonize with the décor of your own home.

The designs in this book are presented as a pathway to develop your skills while discovering the artist within. Each design can be painted as presented, expanded or modified, whatever your preference. To derive the greatest fulfillment, paint to please yourself. You will begin to see your own artistic style emerge as you express your creativity with confidence.

chapter one

MATERIALS

BRUSHES

It is important to invest in the best brushes you can afford. You will only struggle and frustrate yourself if you try to create a masterpiece with cheap brushes. For projects in this book I used Loew-Cornell brushes. Specific types and sizes are listed at the beginning of each project.

To extend the life of your brushes, always treat them with care and clean them thoroughly after each use. Acrylic paint that dries in the brush will cause the brush to become less flexible and create a "fish mouth" where there should be a fine chisel edge. To clean your brushes, I recommend DecoMagic Brush & Jewelry Cleaner by DecoArt. This is a water-based, concentrated cleaner that removes acrylic paints, oil paints and leafing adhesive from your brushes and hands. To avoid potential mishaps, keep this cleaner away from your project. When your painting session is over, work the cleaner in the brush to clean the paint away from the ferrule. Rinse and repeat. Blot the clean brush on a paper towel to make certain there is no color remaining. Shape your clean brushes with soap and lay them flat to dry in order to keep moisture from draining into the ferrule and causing damage.

SPONGE APPLICATORS

4-INCH (10.2CM) SPONGE ROLLER A dense foam roller will quickly basecoat large areas and provide a fine-tooth texture that is ideal for drybrushing.

2-INCH (51MM) SPONGE BRUSH You may need to use a sponge brush for surfaces that aren't flat or to reach into areas that are too tight for a roller. You can produce the same texture as with a roller by patting the paint with the broad side of the sponge brush. To apply color evenly to a rounded edge, use a sponge brush with light, steady pressure.

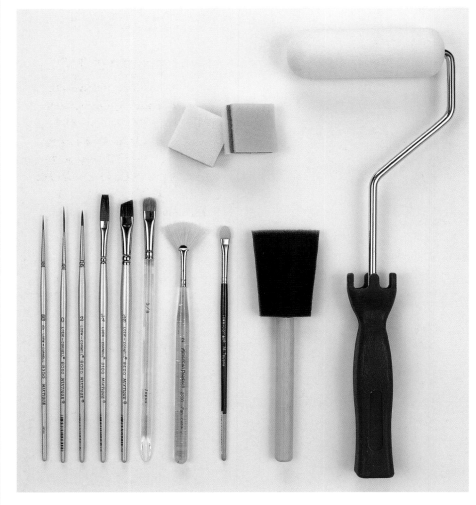

BRUSHES AND SPONGE APPLICATORS
Left to right: liner, script liner, round, lettering, angular, crescent, fan, touche, sponge brush, sponge roller. Above brushes: petit four sponges.

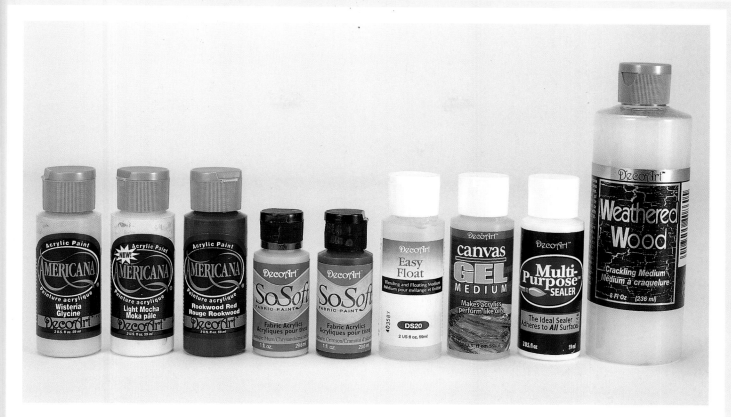

PETIT FOUR SPONGE For surfaces with tight curves and indentations, use a petit four sponge applicator. Pounce the paint onto the surface and walk it out until you have a fine-tooth texture.

SPONGE-TIPPED APPLICATOR For small rounded edges, a sponge-tipped applicator, like those used to apply eye shadow, or a touche by Loew-Cornell, is indispensable.

PAINTS, MEDIUMS & MORE

DECOART AMERICANA BOTTLED ACRYLICS
A variety of colors can be found in many of the large craft chains. However, these stores rarely carry the full line of colors available. I suggest you try your local decorative painting shop where they are usually willing to order any color you need that is not currently in their stock. If you do not

floating TIP

Several thin layers will produce a smoother, more even float than one heavier application of paint.

have a local studio, many of the shops now have Web sites where you can obtain the same personalized service and expert advice.

DECOART SOSOFT FABRIC PAINT This paint is formulated to bond with fabrics and remain pliable when dry. It does not require heat setting or fabric medium

DECOART EASY FLOAT Use Easy Float in your water to facilitate linework, floating and blending on all surfaces except porcelain or glass. Nonporous surfaces do not dry as quickly, and using Easy Float or similar products may result in the paint lifting.

DECOART CANVAS GEL This product was created to extend the drying time of acrylic paints and allow them to be blended like oils. I find it useful to prevent paint drying and clumping in small drybrushes.

DECOART MULTI-PURPOSE SEALER A water-based sealer that works on a variety of surfaces and can be used alone or mixed with paint for basecoating.

drybrushing TIP

Because drybrushing is done without water, acrylic paint may start to dry and clump in the brushes if used for any length of time. To keep paint from drying and to help extend the life of your brush, load the brush first with DecoArt Canvas Gel. Wipe excess gel from the brush and proceed as usual.

When applied to the edges of tape, it helps create crisp, clean lines with no paint bleed.

DECOART WEATHERED WOOD Weathered Wood is a crackling medium that is sandwiched between two layers of paint. Use of this medium causes the top coat of paint to crack, allowing the undercoat to show through.

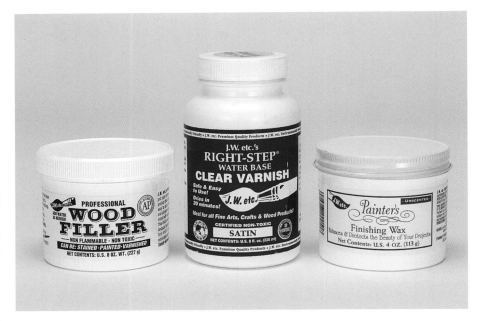

preparation TIPS

• To smooth the rough end grain on wood, combine J.W. etc.'s filler with their First-step sealer to create a sloppy paste. Fill the end grain with the mixture and allow it to dry. You can then sand the ends as smoothly as the top.

• When basecoating wood, I use a sponge roller wherever possible. It's quick and produces a fine eggshell texture without brushstrokes or ridges. To avoid wasting paint between coats, I mist the roller with water from a spray bottle and store it in a zipper bag sealed up to the handle until all basecoating is completed.

• Because I have no way of knowing what products have been used on vintage pieces prior to my acquisition, I prefer to have any "found" objects dip-stripped by a professional refinisher and touch-sanded so that I can begin with a fresh surface. This is especially helpful on surfaces with intricate areas where paint and other finishes may be difficult to remove. Alternatively, remove the old finish from the surface, taking care to follow all precautions as directed by the manufacturer of products you use.

• Commercial furniture makers use a variety of finishes. At the time of purchase, inquire as to the type of finish that was used on the surface you plan to paint. Prior to painting, I consult a professional furniture refinisher to determine the compatibility of the final application with the original finish. After painting I have additional layers of professional grade precatylized lacquer applied to protect the artwork. If you're uncertain about the compatibility of the original finish with the product that you plan to use on the completed surface, have the original finish removed.

J.W. ETC.'S WOOD FILLER When working on wood surfaces you may find nail holes or other dents. These recesses should be filled using J.W. etc.'s Wood Filler. If the filler begins to dry in the container, just moisten it with a few drops of water and stir well. Once the filler dries, it sands easily, creating a smooth surface.

VARNISH

Choosing a finish to protect your paintings is a matter of personal preference. I'm partial to a matte finish and used that on most projects in this book. J.W. etc.'s Right-Step flat matte is water-based, self-leveling, can be wet sanded, and provides a beautiful matte finish like no other. Right-Step is also available in both satin and gloss finishes. To avoid problems that may arise from chemical incompatibility, only combine finishes that are of the same product line and brand.

When applying a brush-on varnish, use a soft brush or painter's pad to eliminate brushstrokes. Pour the varnish into a separate dish to avoid contaminating the entire bottle. Apply several coats, being careful not to let the varnish puddle. Allow each coat to dry thoroughly. Wet sand to remove brushstrokes, and allow the surface to dry completely. Failure to let the surface dry may result in a milky haze trapped between varnish layers.

Apply several more coats of varnish and sand between each coat. Do not sand the final coat. For large or intricate items, wonderful results can be produced with the use of a sprayer.

VARNISHING ALERT!!

Any item that will come in contact with food must be finished with a varnish that is labeled food safe. "Non-toxic" does not mean food safe!

J.W. ETC.'S PAINTER'S FINISHING WAX For added protection and a beautiful luster, apply a coat of Finishing Wax over your varnished project. Allow the varnish to cure for twenty-four hours prior to waxing.

STENCILING MATERIALS

SIMPLY ELEGANT STENCILS BY REBECCA BAER

Simply Elegant Stencils are used to readily achieve the elegant look of free-hand painting with ease. The stencils are also great for custom backgrounds on the pages inside heirloom scrapbooks, like the photo mat project on page 56, when used with acid-free paints. Although not labeled as such, DecoArt's Americana paints are acid-free.

Basic stencil use and care are explained on the packaging. Cleaning information is on this page under "Stencil Cleaners."

STENCIL BRUSHES A variety of stencil brushes are suitable for use with Simply Elegant Stencils, but I find that, due to the intricate nature of the stencils, an exceptionally tightly packed brush or one with an absolutely flat end does not work well because it will not enter the fine openings. I've tried a variety and have found the Loew-Cornell 1150 series to work well. The sizes currently available are $\frac{1}{2}$-inch (13mm) and larger. The large sizes, $1\frac{1}{4}$-inch (32mm) to $1\frac{1}{2}$-inch (38mm), are ideal for filling in the allover background stencils. Typically, when a specific size is listed, any reasonably close size is suitable. For example, a $\frac{3}{4}$-inch (19mm) brush can be used instead of a $\frac{1}{2}$-inch (13mm), and vice versa.

DECOART DECORATING PASTE This is for embossed stenciling. See the sidebar on this page.

STENCIL CLEANERS The type of stencil cleaner you use is determined by your stenciling material, as explained below.

• *Antibacterial hand gel (also called waterless hand cleaner and hand sanitizer)* Used for cleaning acrylic paint from stencils. Due to the intricate detail of Simply Elegant Stencils by Rebecca Baer, they are delicate and must be cleaned carefully. Lay the

embossed stenciling

Embossed stenciling is done with a paste, such as DecoArt Decorating Paste, that leaves a raised design on the surface. Here are a few pointers.

• The stencil must be in full contact with the surface. Any gaps will allow the decorating paste to ooze beneath the stencil. Clean up mistakes on the surface immediately, using the chisel edge of a damp angular or a rubber-tipped wipe-out tool.

• If paste oozes beneath the stencil, you must clean the stencil prior to continuing. Otherwise, you can use the stencil for two to three applications before cleaning.

• Continuation of a design must be delayed until the first application has set up. Ideally, the previous segment should be dry.

• Remember always to clean the stencil immediately after using it for embossing. (See "Pink Soap" on this page.)

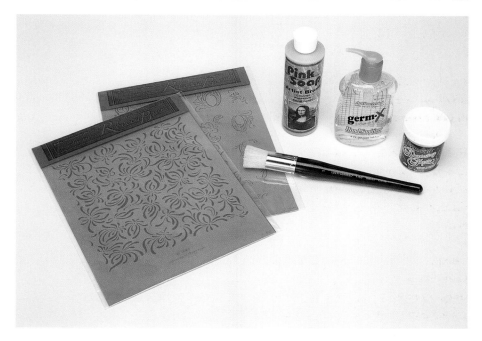

stencil flat on a tray and squirt it with antibacterial hand gel. Gently rub the gel over the stencil with your fingertips to remove the paint. Disperse the gel with liquid soap, rinse well and place the stencil flat on a towel to dry.

• *Pink Soap* This cleaner from Houston Art is used for cleaning decorating paste from stencils. Follow the same cleaning procedure as used with antibacterial hand gel. Always clean this paste from the stencil immediately after use, or the dried paste may ruin the stencil.

Pink Soap is also used as a follow-up after cleaning stencils with antibacterial hand gel and for cleaning brushes.

OTHER COMMON MATERIALS

SANDING PAD For surfaces that require sanding, I use square sanding pads with a sponge backing. They're easy to hold and readily conform to any surface.

TRACING PAPER Tracing paper is available in pads and rolls of varying sizes. I find rolls to be most economical and versatile. I can cut any length desired to fit the pattern or surface. To tear a piece of paper from the roll and still have a straight, clean edge, use an architectural or engineering scale. This looks like a long triangular-shaped ruler. Roll out the desired length of paper on a firm surface and place the scale against the roll on top of the sheet to be torn off. Hold the scale firmly in place and pull the paper from the top against the scale to use it as a cutter. Slide the scale down the roll as needed to tear the sheet.

SOAPSTONE OR CHALK PENCIL A chalk pencil is useful for sketching simple patterns on small surfaces, for re-establishing lost or missing pattern lines and for marking off borders. Marks made with a soapstone pencil are more easily removed but are not as visible as chalk pencil marks.

RULER Your painted lines will be straighter if you use a ruler for both tracing and transferring patterns. You'll also need a ruler for measuring borders and surfaces.

TRANSFER PAPER To transfer patterns, I prefer to use either Saral white transfer paper or blue Super Chacopaper.

Saral is wax free, so marks can be erased easily or wiped away with a damp cloth. The only exceptions are when you have trapped lines under a thin layer of paint or when you have transferred a pattern too soon after you've basecoated the surface. Transferring a pattern immediately after the basecoating results in the lines being cured into the paint, making the pattern impossible to remove.

Chacopaper is water-soluble, which makes it handy for surfaces where erasing over delicate layers may create a light spot. You can remove pattern lines by simply dampening and blotting the surface. The surface may be dampened numerous times to remove stubborn lines, but you should allow the surface to dry each time to avoid softening and lifting the paint. New chaco may be very intense in color. To ease removal from the completed project, you may wish to wipe down the chacopaper with a dry paper towel prior to using. To extend the life of chacopaper, keep it in a plastic bag so it won't fade from exposure to humidity.

STYLUS Choose a stylus with ball ends, typically of two different sizes. The stylus is used for transferring patterns and creating small dots.

PALETTE PAPER A neutral gray disposable palette will make it easier for you to accurately assess the value of colors you are working with, especially when

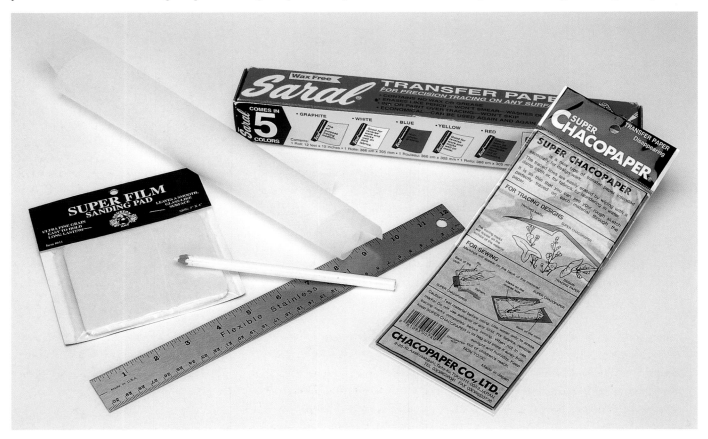

creating mixes. A gray palette also facilitates proper blending of light-value colors on your brush.

PALETTE KNIFE A narrow palette knife is the most versatile for mixing paints. It will mix small amounts of paint on your palette and will fit into a paint bottle for stirring. A palette knife with an angled blade, such as a J-20, is more suitable for spreading paste over a stencil to create an embossed image, such as on the lampshade cover on page 42.

PAPER TOWELS You'll need absorbent paper towels to blot excess water from

taping TIP

To maintain a clean edge when separating colors with tape, press the edge of the tape firmly in place and seal the edge with Multi-Purpose Sealer. Allow the sealer to dry and apply the desired paint color. This works especially well when you want to tape an area that has been sponged, stenciled or has multiple paint colors, and it is impractical to seal the tape with a single basecoat color.

your brush after rinsing. Soft paper towels such as Viva by Kleenex draw just the right amount of moisture out of the brush for blending and floating.

BRUSH BASIN A brush basin is preferable to a water container because a basin has molded brush rests that suspend the brush and keep the bristles from touching the basin bottom and becoming distorted. A basin also has ridges to help vibrate paint from the brush. The ferrule, not the bristles, should be pulled across the ridges.

KNEADED ERASER A kneaded eraser removes pencil and pattern lines without damaging the surface and can be shaped to fit small areas.

MAGIC RUB ERASER A vinyl eraser is non-abrasive and non-smudging, and can be angled with a craft knife to fit small areas.

MASKING TAPE Masking tape is available in several sizes, and by combining them, you can create borders of various widths without measuring. I keep $^3/_4$-inch (19mm), $^1/_2$-inch (13mm), $^1/_4$-inch (6mm) and $^1/_8$-inch (3mm) on hand.

basic supplies

In the project supply lists you'll see references to "basic supplies." These painting supplies, used for almost every project, include the following:
- brush basin
- palette paper
- palette knife
- transfer paper
- tracing paper
- paper towels
- stylus
- brush cleaner

The more narrow tapes are located with quilting notions in sewing stores and with graphic supplies at office supply stores. Masking tape can be stretched gently to conform to curves. As a rule of thumb, the narrower the tape, the more readily it conforms to curves without puckering.

Individual projects may call for other supplies not mentioned in this chapter. These are included in the project supply lists.

chapter two

GENERAL TECHNIQUES

TRACING, ENLARGING & REDUCING THE PATTERN

Generally, your project will begin with a pattern. Tracing the pattern may seem to be tedious, busy work, but in reality, each pattern you trace becomes a drawing lesson. By tracing the patterns instead of photocopying them, you will become familiar not only with one arrangement but also with the various elements that make up that design.

The design sense gained from tracing comes in handy when you want to use a pattern on a surface other than the one shown. To adapt a pattern, begin by tracing an outline of the surface you would like to use. The outline will establish the boundaries for the design. If the pattern is the proper size, you can simply arrange the various elements as desired and trace them. If the surface is either larger or smaller than the original pattern, you will need to adjust the size on a copier.

The easiest way to determine the percentage at which the pattern will need to be run is to divide the final size by the original size. For example, if you want to take a pattern that is 6" (15.2cm) wide and enlarge it to 12" (30.5cm), you begin with the final size of 12" (30.5), divide it by the original six of 6" (15.2cm) and get a result of 2. Multiply this answer by 100 and you get your enlargement percentage of 200. The same formula works for reducing. If you want to make a 12" (30.5cm) pattern fit a 6" (15.2cm) surface, begin again with the final size of 6" (15.2cm), divide it by the original size of 12" (30.5cm) and multiply the result of .5 by 100 to get 50%.

FORMULA FOR SIZING PATTERNS

$$\frac{\text{final size}}{\text{original size}} \times 100 = \text{photocopier \%}$$

TRANSFERRING THE PATTERN

Once you've sized and traced your pattern, you're ready to transfer it to your project surface.

transferring TIP

To keep track of where you have transferred your pattern, cover the traced pattern with a piece of waxed paper. As you transfer, the completed areas will appear as white lines on the waxed paper. You will not lose your place, even if you need to stop in mid-transfer.

TRANSFERRING THE PATTERN TO A FIRM SURFACE

Place the pattern on the project surface in the desired position and secure it with removable (low-tack) tape to prevent shifting. Slip a sheet of transfer paper under the pattern. Using a ball-tip stylus, trace over the design. Before removing the tape, lift a corner of the pattern and transfer paper to make sure the traced pattern is complete.

TRANSFERRING THE PATTERN TO FABRIC

When transferring a pattern to fabric, you may find that a stylus will tear the tracing paper. To protect and extend the life of the pattern, cover the traced pattern with clear Con-Tact paper. This will allow the pattern to be used many times over without significant damage.

FINDING THE CENTER OF A SURFACE

Positioning lettering or other design elements often starts with finding the center of a surface.

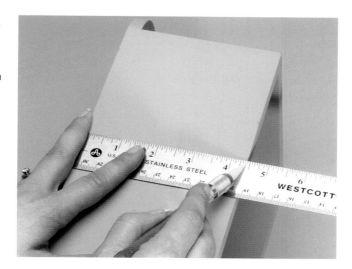

1 | MEASURE THE SURFACE

When measuring for the center or a centerline, you may find that your chosen surface does not come to a measurement that is easily divided in half, such as the one shown here.

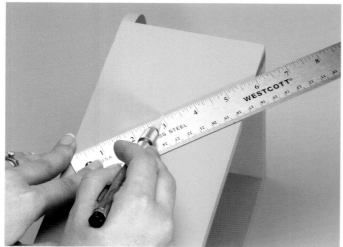

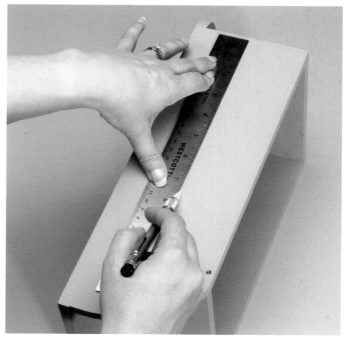

2 | ANGLE THE RULER

To find the center, begin by placing your ruler at an angle across one end of the surface so the measurement is easily divisible by two. Here I've angled the ruler so the overall measurement is 6". Mark the halfway point, which in this case is 3".

In the same manner, angle the ruler at the opposite end of the surface. Again, mark the halfway point. The number shown on the ruler is irrelevant. It simply must be readily divisible by two.

3 | DRAW THE CENTERLINE

Draw your centerline by connecting the marks, as shown.

CREATING ACCURATE MIXES

The best method for creating a paint mix depends on the quantity of paint you want to mix.

SMALL QUANTITIES

Most of your paint mixes need to be created only in small quantities. To do this, measure your proportions in drops, as shown on the right.

LARGE QUANTITIES

Sometimes you need larger quantities of mixed paint, such as when you're basecoating a surface. To create large quantities of paint mixes accurately, you need the following:

- empty, clean paint bottle
- adhesive-backed label
- ruler and marker
- narrow palette knife

Then follow the steps in the illustrations to the right.

BRUSH MIXES

A combination of colors followed by +/- means that you should adjust the value of the color using more or less of the second color as needed for visibility. Each time we paint something, it will vary slightly. When you are painting something like a center vein on a leaf, a 1:1 mix might work on some leaves, while other leaves may need a 2:1 or 1:2 ratio in order to be visible. Just brush-mix the value desired using the colors listed.

1 SMALL QUANTITY MIX
To create a 2:1:1 mixture, squeeze two equally sized drops of the first color listed onto your palette paper. Then squeeze one drop *of the same size* of the next color, followed by one drop *of the same size* of the last color.

2 Combine the three colors with your palette knife.

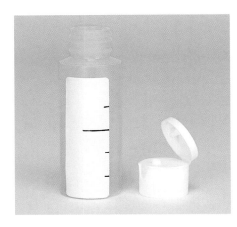

1 LARGE QUANTITY MIX
Using a ruler, apply lines at measured intervals to an adhesive-backed label. Make sure you have enough lines to accommodate the proportions for your mix. In other words, to create a 3:1 mixture, you need four lines. Adhere the label to a clean paint bottle, being careful to line up the edge of the label with the bottom of the bottle.

2 Pour the first color listed into your paint bottle until it is filled to the third line (three parts).

3 Add the second color until the level reaches the fourth line (one part). Shake well or stir with a narrow palette knife.

SPATTERING

By using a fan brush and palette knife to spatter, you can control the placement and direction of the spatters with reasonable accuracy, as shown below.

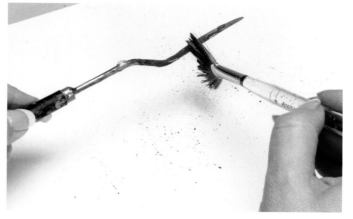

1 First thin the paint to an ink-like consistency. Then pick up the thinned paint on a stiff fan brush. Place the brush on the palette knife and begin to apply pressure.

2 As you continue to apply pressure, move the loaded brush downward across the edge of the palette knife to create spatters on the surface. For the best results, always spatter your palette paper first to check the size of the spatters before moving to your project. Large spatters indicate a brush too heavily loaded. To reduce the load, lightly blot the brush on a paper towel.

BUILDING A THIN-LINE HIGHLIGHT

Several projects in this book call for building a highlight on a thin line, such as a tendril or the individual wires of an eggbeater.

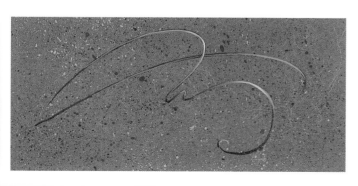

1 Begin by establishing the line with the darkest value.

2 Build forward areas by creating a slightly lighter value and painting over the segment that you wish to bring to the forefront.

3 Next, further lighten the value and paint a shorter segment within the previous application. For the lightest areas, touch a small highlight on the most forward section.

chapter three

LETTERING TECHNIQUES

Every lettering project requires choosing a lettering design style, or font. The fonts I used for projects in this book come from *100 Ornamental Alphabets* and *Victorian Display Alphabets*, both books by Dan X. Solo, published by Dover Publications. Even with a designed font, you may go through a process of adjustments and design decisions, such as are discussed in this chapter.

CHANGING THE WEIGHT OF THE LETTERING

Sometimes the lettering font you select for a project is stylistically appropriate but not the right weight.

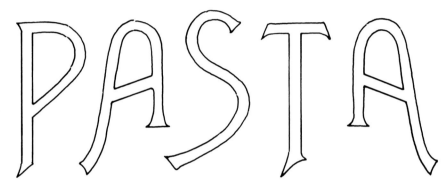

I felt this "Art Gothic" font from *100 Ornamental Alphabets* was a good choice for the first project in this book, which involves etching lettering on glass. Note that the font has a uniform thickness or "weight" that is clean and simple for ease of cutting. However, the font is narrow, and it may be lost in the subtlety of the tone-on-tone effect created by the etching.

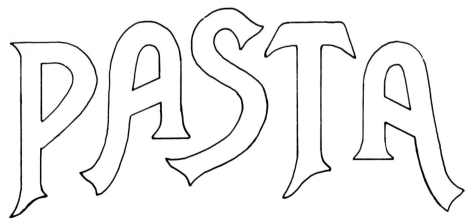

To increase the weight of the font, I added $\frac{1}{16}$" (1.6mm) on all sides. Adding an equal amount on all sides allows me to maintain the visual balance of the letters. To add $\frac{1}{8}$" (3mm) along one or two sides would cause the text to appear uneven.

ADDING EMBELLISHMENTS

For the magazine box project (pages 98-107), I chose the font "Eureka" from *100 Ornamental Alphabets* and then embellished the lettering with a border and a bittersweet vine.

In the above example, the bittersweet vine flows throughout the lettering, resulting in a cluttered, confusing design.

By moving the bittersweet beyond the perimeter of the box, the text remains the focus and is clearly readable, while the bittersweet provides an attractive accent.

ADAPTING TEXT TO A ROUND SURFACE

Although I have not used any round surfaces for projects in this book, you may want to adapt my designs or create your own designs for just such a shape. The illustrations below show the process used to develop text on a curve. Beginning with a loose spiral, I placed the body of the text, using the font "Ringlet" from *Victorian Display Alphabets*.

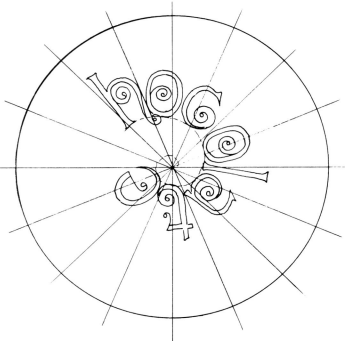

SPIRALING TEXT

The spiral is not tight enough to be evident and could appear to be a poorly done circle. Note that when determining the plan for the body of the word, I did not include the initial "C."

TIGHTENING THE SPIRAL

Here the spiral is tighter than in the first image. In spite of this, it becomes apparent that a single word is too short to spiral effectively. Time to abandon the spiral for a simple curve.

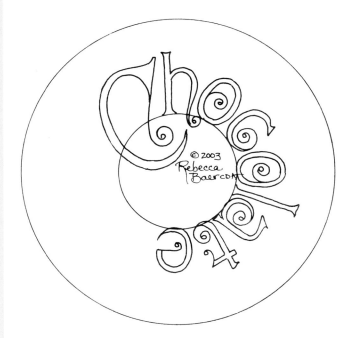

CURVING TEXT

In order to develop the text on a curve, you need a compass to establish an arc. Here I have simply drawn a smaller circle within the larger one, which is the boundary of my surface. The round surface can be turned and viewed from any direction, so there is no need to center the text. On the other hand, a vertical centerline through each letter is helpful for layout. The individual centerlines should all point to the axis of the circle.

Using the same font in a larger size for the first letter helps to create a definite focal point. This layout could be finished off with a curving decorative border.

Another approach to the round surface is to put the text straight across the middle.

STAGGERED TEXT

Here I used the font "Recherche" from *Victorian Display Alphabets*. In order to avoid visually cutting the surface in half, I staggered the lettering with some overlap. This treatment shortens the overall length of the word while taking up more vertical space. It also allows adequate space above and below the text for additional decoration.

designing TIP

Designing is not bound by a formula. It is a matter of trial and error. Follow your creative impulse and explore the possibilities.

STRAIGHT TEXT

In this example I used the font "Pamela" from *Victorian Display Alphabets*.

By making the initial "C" considerably larger than the remaining text, I'm able to move that letter into the background without losing it behind the remaining letters. This creates room to shift the text to the left and into the opening of the initial "C."

In it's original form, "Pamela" has outlines around the individual letters. Removing the individual outlines and unifying them in a single block allows me to squeeze the text into a shorter space.

This design makes good use of the space and would be equally attractive painted as is or further enhanced with additional decoration in the open areas.

GLASS JARS
Etching on Glass

Etching glass is a cost-effective way to create stylish home accessories. It doesn't require prior knowledge of color or any painting experience, and you need only minimal supplies. The process shown here genuinely etches the glass, creating a usable item with a permanent design. The subtle tone-on-tone pattern can be done on any plain glass surface and is particularly beautiful on colored glass. One note of caution: sometimes what appears to be colored glass is actually clear glass with a plastic or sprayed-on finish. This prohibits the etching creme from coming in contact with the glass surface, making it unsuitable for this technique.

materials

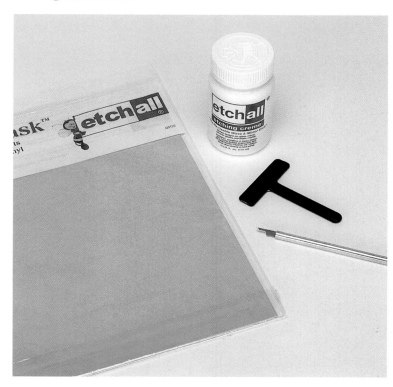

SURFACE
Glass jars, available from from Painter's Paradise
    tall: item 360093
    medium: item 360092
    small: item 360091

ETCHALL SUPPLIES
- Etchall Etchmask 8" × 11" (20.3cm × 27.9cm) vinyl sheets
- Etchall Etching Creme
- Etchall squeegee
- Etchall pick knife

ADDITIONAL SUPPLIES
- Tracing paper
- Wide, flexible ruler
- Towel (optional)
- Tape
- Transfer paper
- Stylus
- Small piece of clean nylon stocking

For font identification and help in finding supplies, see Resources on page 126.

PATTERNS

These patterns may be hand-traced or photocopied for personal use only. Enlarge at 167 percent to bring up to full size.

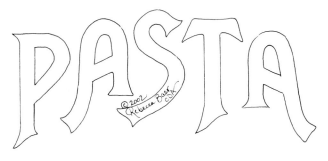

1 **PREPARATION FOR ETCHING**

Trace the pattern onto tracing paper and set aside. Make sure the surface to be etched is clean, dry and free of any residue. To mask the surface, apply a sheet of Etchmask to the glass. Do not substitute Con-Tact paper. Begin on one side and remove the backing with one hand as you use the other hand to smooth the vinyl onto the glass with the squeegee. Work slowly and carefully to avoid creating wrinkles or trapping air bubbles beneath the vinyl. Do not discard the backing paper at this time.

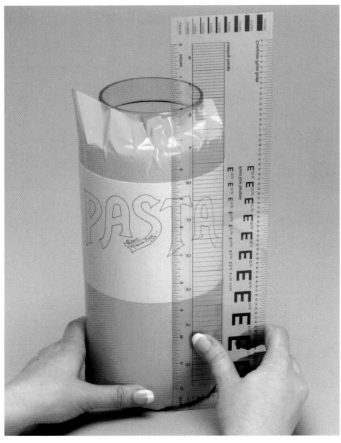

2 Carefully position the traced pattern over the vinyl. To make sure the text is straight, rest a drafting triangle, carpenter's square or a wide ruler (such as I'm using here) on a tabletop to line up the vertical segments of the letters and position the pattern. Secure the pattern with tape.

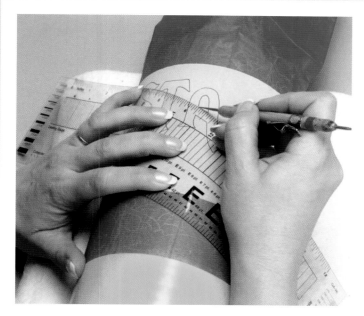

3   Slip a sheet of transfer paper between the pattern and the vinyl. Using a stylus, transfer the pattern to the vinyl. A flexible ruler enables you to transfer the straight lines more accurately. Remove the traced pattern.

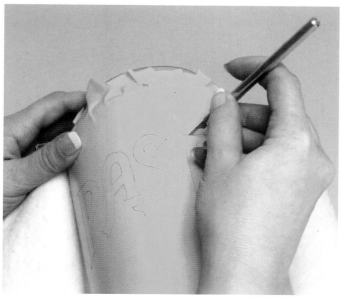

4   Using a pick knife, cut the design into the vinyl. Hold the knife perpendicular to the surface and cut using only the tip of the blade. Ideally, you should try to cut each continuous line in a single pass to avoid overlaps from starting and stopping.

5   When an outline is completely cut, you can remove the vinyl letter. To do this, make a small slit in the area that you wish to remove. Then catch the vinyl at the slit on the tip of the knife and gently lift out the section. Do not try to catch the piece that you wish to remove by working along an edge, because this damages the clean, sharp edge of the letter. Continue until the entire pattern has been cut out. To keep the glass clean and free from fingerprints, avoid touching the areas where you've removed the vinyl.

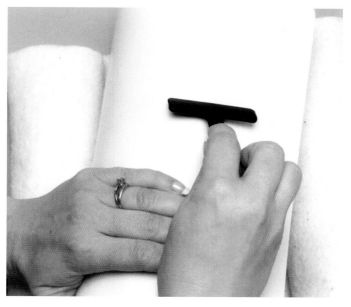

6   Place the Etchall vinyl sheet backing paper over the cut pattern and, using the squeegee, burnish to secure all edges of the design.

etching TIP

To prevent the jar from rolling as you work, place a towel on the table and roll both ends to form a channel in the middle for the jar.

7 | Check the design for flaws and cut away any tails. The vinyl must be tightly adhered without irregularities to produce a clean image.

8 | Hold the image up to light to see if there is any residual adhesive on the glass. Remove adhesive by rubbing it with a piece of clean nylon stocking. DO NOT USE GLASS CLEANER, which will destroy the adhesive properties of the vinyl. Cover with Etchmask vinyl any exposed areas of glass that you don't wish to etch.

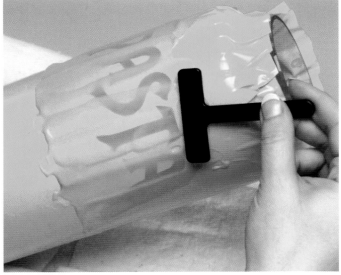

9 | **ETCHING THE DESIGN**
Pour a generous amount of etching creme on the vinyl where the pattern is not exposed.

10 | Using the squeegee, spread the creme over the design all at once, extending the creme beyond the cut area. DO NOT USE A BRUSH.

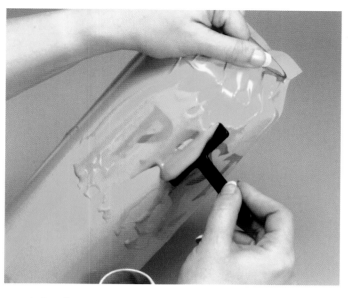 

11 Let the creme stand on the surface, untouched, for 15 minutes. Then use the squeegee to remove the creme from the surface.

12 Return the etching creme to the jar for reuse. Although once exposed to air the creme will darken with age, this does not reduce its effectiveness. Rinse the surface thoroughly under running water. Take care not to allow any creme that is flushing off to run onto exposed glass, which would cloud the glass and cause streaks. Remove the vinyl by running water between the pattern and the glass as you pull the vinyl from the surface. Wash and dry the surface.

VINTAGE STYLE MAILBOX
Establishing Focus With Upper and Lower Case

This charming glass mailbox calls images of yesteryear to mind and would be an eye-catching receptacle for just about anything, including incoming or outgoing mail. To harmonize with the vintage appearance, I chose to create a randomly crackled background combined with a label of Victorian-style lettering. A touch of stenciled scrollwork to balance the lettering and a no-prep surface make this an attractive project that can be completed fairly quickly.

colors and materials

PAINT: DecoArt Americana Acrylics

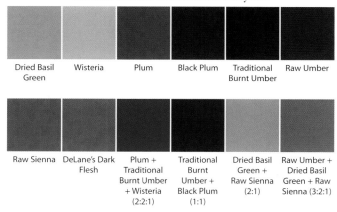

Dried Basil Green	Wisteria	Plum	Black Plum	Traditional Burnt Umber	Raw Umber

Raw Sienna	DeLane's Dark Flesh	Plum + Traditional Burnt Umber + Wisteria (2:2:1)	Traditional Burnt Umber + Black Plum (1:1)	Dried Basil Green + Raw Sienna (2:1)	Raw Umber + Dried Basil Green + Raw Sienna (3:2:1)

SURFACE
Glass mailbox with metal lid item 811200 from Painter's Paradise

LOEW-CORNELL BRUSHES
- Mixtique round, series 8000, no. 3/0
- Mixtique script liner, series 8050, no. 0
- Mixtique lettering, series 8100, ⅛-inch (3mm)
- Stencil brush, series 1150, ½-inch (13mm)

ADDITIONAL SUPPLIES
- Basic supplies (See page 13.)
- DecoArt Weathered Wood crackle medium
- DecoArt Easy Float (See page 9.)
- Petit four sponge
- White transfer paper
- Low-tack tape
- Stencil ST-104 Renaissance Corners & Borders, Simply Elegant Stencils from Rebecca Baer, Inc.
- Antibacterial hand gel
- Pink Soap
- Varnish (See page 33, step 16.)

For font identification and help in finding supplies, see Resources on page 126.

PATTERN

This pattern may be hand-traced or photocopied for personal use only. This pattern is at full size.

1 **CRACKLED BACKGROUND**
Using a dry petit four sponge, apply random patches of Weathered Wood to the outer lid on the mailbox. Don't cover completely. The Weathered Wood will create a crackle effect when you apply the topcoat. Allow the surface to dry or quick dry with a hair dryer.

2 Combine Plum + Traditional Burnt Umber + Wisteria (2:2:1). Using a damp petit four sponge, apply the paint mixture to the outer lid. Thinner areas of application produce smaller, finer cracks, while heavier areas produce larger cracks. Do not go back over any portion of the topcoat once it has been sponged. In addition, do not quick dry the topcoat; it must air dry to produce the cracks.

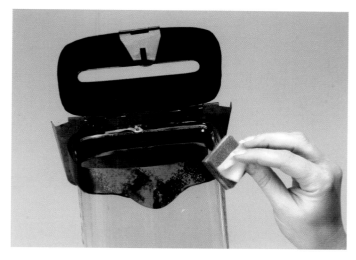

3 | **METAL BAND AND SECONDARY LID**
Using a damp petit four sponge, apply random patches of Plum + Traditional Burnt Umber + Wisteria (2:2:1) to the metal band and latch. Allow areas of the background to remain visible along with the patches of sponged color. Don't be concerned about getting paint on the glass. It will wipe off easily with a damp paper towel.

4 | Combine Traditional Burnt Umber + Black Plum (1:1) and, without completely covering the existing colors, apply random patches to the metal band and latch. Continue onto the secondary lid in just a few of the sparse areas.

5 | **LETTERING**
Transfer the lettering pattern to the lid (see page 14.) Using a ⅛-inch (3mm) lettering brush, apply the main body of the word "LETTER" using DeLane's Dark Flesh.

6 | Apply extensions with a no. 3/0 round.

7 | Highlight the body of the "L" with horizontal lines of Dried Basil Green + Raw Sienna (2:1) on a no. 0 script liner. Group the lines closely at the top of the letter and increase spacing as you progress downward. Outline each letter with the same mix and brush.

8   Using a ⅛-inch (3mm) lettering brush, apply the main body of the word "post" using Raw Umber + Dried Basil Green + Raw Sienna (3:2:1). Apply extensions with a no. 3/0 round.

9   Apply Dried Basil Green + Raw Sienna (2:1) in the center of the wider sections of "post" with a no. 3/0 round.

10   **STENCILING**
The stencil may be used whole or cut apart for manageability, if desired. Position the rounded corner from stencil ST-104 on the lower right of the lid, as shown, and secure on the underside with loops of tape.

11   Pick up Black Plum on a dry ½-inch (13mm) stencil brush and wipe on a paper towel to remove excess paint. Pounce over the corner until the scrollwork is filled in.

12   Shift the stencil up and to the right just a hair. Secure the stencil with tape. Without rinsing the brush, add DeLane's Dark Flesh. Wipe the brush again on a paper towel to lightly blend the colors and remove the excess paint. Pounce over the corner again until the scrollwork is filled in. A hairline shadow of the Black Plum will remain on the lower left of the DeLane's Dark Flesh.

13　Without moving the stencil, carefully lift its corner to check visibility. If you would like for the scrollwork to be more noticeable, pick up additional DeLane's Dark Flesh on the brush, wipe the brush on a paper towel to remove excess paint and pounce again. If the scrollwork can be adequately distinguished from the background, proceed to highlight the scrollwork as explained in the next step.

14　Without rinsing the brush, pick up Dried Basil Green, wipe to remove excess, and then pounce selected patches of the scrollwork to highlight.

　　When done, remove the stencil, to see completed scrollwork with a slender shadow and subtle highlighting as shown in the photos below.

15　Position the central motif from ST-104 on the forward half of the secondary lid with the flat edge of the motif facing the mail slot. Refer to steps 11 through 14 and, in the same manner, apply the stenciled scrollwork to the secondary lid. Due to its intricate detail, the stencil must be cleaned carefully. Refer to the instructions under "Stencil Cleaners" on page 11.

16　A simple coat of matte spray may best preserve the vintage appearance of the mailbox. However, if you plan to use the mailbox outside, this will not offer adequate protection. To provide sufficient protection for outdoor use, you will need to apply several coats of exterior varnish to the lid.

ACCENT TABLE
Beautifying Furniture

Won't you come into the garden? I would like my roses to see you.
ROBERT BRINSLEY SHERIDAN

This delightful porringer-style end table is an antique reproduction, which makes it readily available. The beautiful tiger maple comes with a light finish already applied. Commercial furniture makers use a variety of finishes, so at the time of purchasing this piece, I inquired as to the type of finish that was used. Then, prior to painting, I consulted a professional furniture refinisher, who determined that additional finishing layers of professional-grade precatylized lacquer would be compatible with the original finish. After painting, I had the additional layers of lacquer applied to protect the artwork. If you are uncertain about the compatibility of the original finish with the product that you plan to use on the completed table, have the original finish removed.

colors and materials

PAINT: DecoArt Americana Acrylics

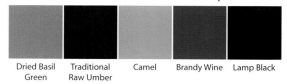

| Dried Basil Green | Traditional Raw Umber | Camel | Brandy Wine | Lamp Black |

SURFACE
Tiger maple porringer-style end table from Little's Antiques & Reproductions

LOEW-CORNELL BRUSHES
- Mixtique filbert, series 8500, no. 6
- Mixtique round, series 8000, no. 2
- Mixtique script liner, series 8050, no. 0
- Stencil brush, series 1150, ¹/₂-inch (13mm)

ADDITIONAL SUPPLIES
- Basic supplies (See page 13.)
- Fine nylon sanding pad
- White transfer paper
- Stencil ST-108 Motifs & Medallions, Simply Elegant Stencils from Rebecca Baer, Inc.
- Low-tack tape
- DecoArt Easy Float (See page 9.)
- Antibacterial hand gel
- Pink Soap
- Sanford Peel-off Magic Rub vinyl eraser
- Varnish (See page 40, step 17.)

For font identification and help in finding supplies, see Resources on page 126.

Won't you come into the garden? I would like my roses to see you.

Robert Brinsley Sheridan
1751–1816

© 2003 Rebecca Baer CDA

PATTERNS

These patterns may be hand-traced or photocopied for personal use only. Enlarge the lettering pattern at 200 percent. The rose pattern is at full size.

© 2003 Rebecca Baer CDA

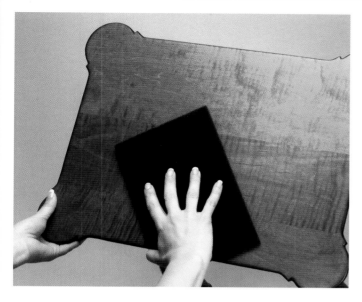

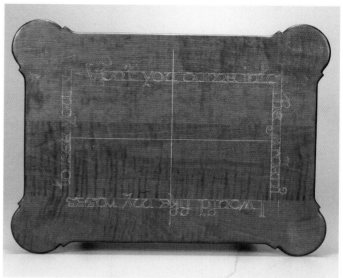

1 SURFACE PREPARATION
If your end table has a finish, determine whether you should remove it (see project introduction, page 35). If you decide to keep the finish, it must be scuffed with a fine nylon sanding pad.

2 Find the center of your surface (see page 15) and establish both a horizontal and a vertical centerline. Use the centerlines to position the pattern on the painting surface. Use a ruler to confirm that the text is both centered and level. Then transfer the lettering onto the table with white transfer paper and your stylus. Although the stenciling must be completed before painting the lettering, it is helpful to have the lettering pattern in place to aid in positioning the stencil.

3 STENCILING
Using the pattern as a guide, position stencil ST-108, motif A on the capital "W" outline, as shown, and tape it in place. Pick up Dried Basil Green on a dry ½-inch (13mm) stencil brush and wipe it on a paper towel to remove excess paint. Pounce over the motif until the scrollwork is filled in.

4 Position motif J just below the completed motif A, and stencil as directed in step 3.

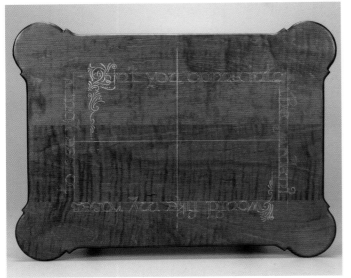

5 | In the same manner, position motif J on the capital "I" outline on the tabletop and complete the stenciling as directed in step 3. Due to its intricate detail, the stencil must be cleaned carefully. Refer to instructions under "Stencil Cleaners" on page 11.

6 | **LETTERING**
Using a no. 2 round brush, apply the lettering, using Lamp Black. (See completed lettering on page 41.)

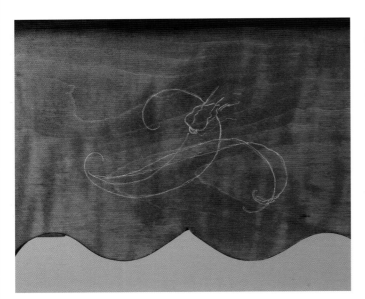

7 | **ROSEBUDS AND TENDRILS**
Using white transfer paper and your stylus, lightly transfer the pattern for the rosebuds on the front and back panels of the table skirting.

8 | Using a no. 6 filbert, undercoat the rosebuds and calyxes with Dried Basil Green.

9 | Place a small puddle each of Traditional Raw Umber, Dried Basil Green and Camel on your palette. Using a no. 0 script liner, brush-mix Traditional Raw Umber + Dried Basil Green, allowing the colors to remain under-blended to create variety. Apply the large tendril that curls behind the rose.

10 | Blend additional Dried Basil Green into the brush and apply a second tendril. In the same manner, blend additional Dried Basil Green into the brush and apply the third tendril. Now blend a touch of Camel into the brush to lighten the color further. Apply the stem of the rosebud.

11 | Build light areas on the stem and tendrils to bring various segments forward. First slightly lighten the stem or tendril color with a touch of Dried Basil Green. Paint over the portion of the tendril or stem you want to bring forward. Then further lighten the value with additional Dried Basil Green and paint a shorter segment within the previous one. For the lightest areas, add a touch of Camel to the dirty brush and paint the smallest highlight of the stem or tendril. See "Building a Thin-line Highlight," page 17, for a closer view of this technique.

12 | Load a no. 6 filbert with Camel and touch one edge of the brush into Brandy Wine to pick up a hint of color. Stroke the brush on your palette to blend the paint until there is a smooth transition of color. Position the brush with the light side to the top of the bud and, using the tip of the brush, daub in the suggestion of a back petal.

13 Now place the tip of the brush at the base of the bud and apply light pressure until the bristles spread enough to fill the rounded base of the bud.

14 Pull the brush toward the top of the bud as you decrease pressure, allowing the bristles to narrow. Rotate the brush one-quarter turn as you finish the bud to create a narrow tip.

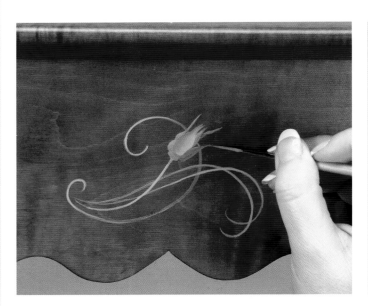

15 Using a no. 0 script liner, brush-mix Traditional Raw Umber + Dried Basil Green, allowing the colors to remain under-blended to create variety. Apply the large calyxes surrounding the rosebud.

16 Allow the painting to dry thoroughly before attempting to remove any remaining pattern lines. Work carefully around the painted area using a vinyl drafting eraser cut at an angle to lift any visible lines. Because the painting is over a layer of varnish, it is delicate and will be susceptible to scratches until the table receives a topcoat.

17 Unless you are working on unfinished wood, any varnish you use must be compatible with the original finish. I took my completed table to a professional furniture refinisher to apply a commercial-grade precatylized lacquer that would not react with the original finish. Ask for the finish to be tested in an inconspicuous area prior to coating the entire table.

ACCENT TABLE: TOP

ACCENT TABLE: FRONT PANEL

LAMPSHADE COVER

Creating a Fresh Look for a Lamp

BEAUTIFUL FLOWER

flor bonita (PORTUGUESE)　　*belle fleur* (FRENCH)　　*fiore bello* (ITALIAN)

This easy-to-make lampshade cover is constructed from polystyrene. The design is painted on the lampshade prior to assembling it, allowing you to paint on a flat surface. The subdued gold background provides subtle support for the lettering, which says "beautiful flower" in three languages—Portuguese, French and Italian. The embossed stenciling is the crowning touch.

This project allows you to give a fresh, new look to your lamps and your room in a matter of seconds by simply slipping the cover over an existing shade.

colors and materials

PAINT: DecoArt Americana Acrylics

| Antique White | Dried Basil Green | Traditional Raw Umber | Raw Sienna | Brandy Wine | Dried Basil Green + Raw Sienna (2:1) |

SURFACE
.20 mil polystyrene, 11" × 17" (27.9cm × 43.2 cm) from Milmar Plastics

LOEW-CORNELL BRUSHES
- Mixtique angular, series 8400, ³/₄-inch (19mm)
- Mixtique script liner, series 8050, no. 0
- American Painter bristle fan, series 2200, no. 2

ADDITIONAL SUPPLIES
- Basic supplies (See page 13.)
- Dense foam roller
- DecoArt Decorating Paste
- Stencil ST-108 Motifs & Medallions, Simply Elegant Stencils from Rebecca Baer, Inc.
- Low-tack tape
- Pink Soap
- Saral white transfer paper
- Kneaded eraser

- Ultra Sticky Craft Tape, ¹/₄-inch (6mm) width
- Craft knife
- 18" (45.7cm) beaded fringe
- 18" (45.7cm) narrow trim of choice for bottom edge of lampshade
- 9" (22.9cm) ¹/₄-inch (6mm) single-fold bias tape

For font identification and help in finding supplies, see Resources on page 126.

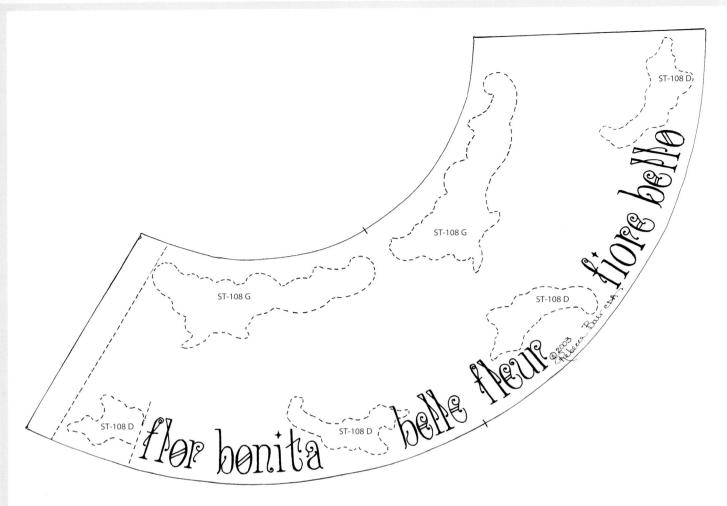

fiore bello

ST-108 D

ST-108 G

ST-108 G

ST-108 D

belle fleur

ST-108 D

ST-108 D

flor bonita

©2003 Rebecca Baer CDA

PATTERN

This pattern may be hand-traced or photocopied for personal use only. Enlarge at 167 percent to bring up to full size.

1 PREPARATION AND EMBOSSED STENCILING

Trace the pattern outline for the shade onto polystyrene and cut it out using scissors. Using a dense sponge roller, basecoat the surface with Dried Basil Green + Raw Sienna (2:1).

Tint about 1 tablespoon of DecoArt Decorating Paste with Antique White. Do not exceed the manufacturer's recommended ratio of 20% paint to 80% paste. Position the stencil on the lampshade as indicated on the pattern. Mask any adjacent areas of stencil with low-tack tape.

paste TIP

Decorating paste dries quickly and will begin to obstruct the stencil openings after only one or two applications. Clean the stencil frequently during use and immediately when finished.

2 | Holding the stencil firmly in place, use the palette knife to gently spread a thin layer of tinted paste over the stencil. Take care to cover all openings but do not use excessive pressure, which could force the paste under the stencil.

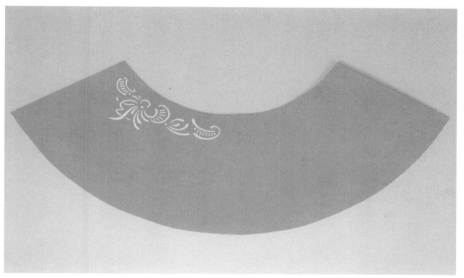

3 | Carefully lift the stencil and set the lampshade aside until the paste is firm. Smudges or small mistakes can be repaired immediately with the chisel edge of a clean, damp angular brush. Clean the stencil while the paste is still wet, using water and Pink Soap. Due to its intricate detail, the stencil is delicate and must be cleaned carefully. Lay the stencil flat on a tray and squirt it with Pink Soap. Gently rub the soap over the stencil with your fingertips to remove the paste. Rinse the stencil well and lay it flat on a towel to dry.

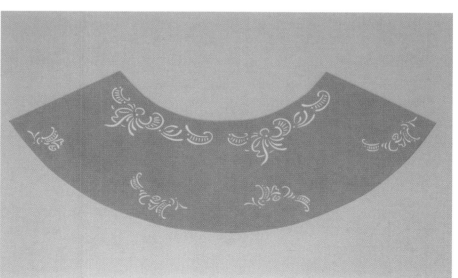

4 | Ideally, the decorating paste should be completely dry, but you can proceed carefully after the paste in the first segment has set up enough not to be damaged. Refer to steps 1 through 3 and repeat the procedure as necessary to complete the embossed scrollwork.

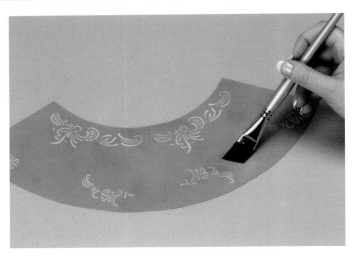

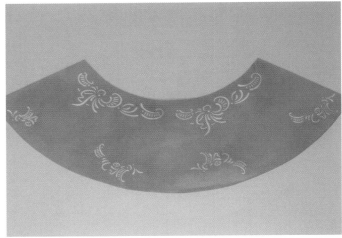

5 **MOTTLING**
Create the mottled background by applying random patches of color, using a slip-slap motion (a series of random overlapping "Xs"). Each color should be applied at wash consistency. The first application must be allowed to dry prior to adding the next color. Patches of color should vary in size and shape with arbitrary overlap and should continue over the embossed stenciling.

First, apply just a hint of Raw Sienna using a side-loaded ¾-inch (19mm) angular. Take care to fade each patch of color around its edges, using the water side of the brush.

6 In the same manner, add patches of Brandy Wine.

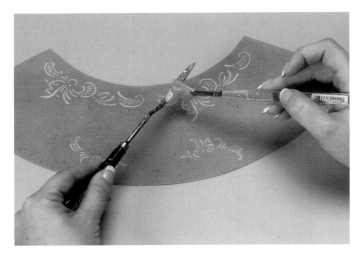

7 **SPATTERING**
Spatter the shade first with Traditional Raw Umber and then repeat using Dried Basil Green. To do this, thin the paint to an ink-like consistency. Then pick up the thinned paint on a no. 2 bristle fan and drag the loaded brush away from you across a palette knife with the bristles facing the surface to be spattered (see page 17).

8 **LETTERING**
Transfer the pattern for the lettering using white transfer paper and a stylus. Paint the letters with Traditional Raw Umber. Thin the paint to an ink-like consistency and apply it with a no. 0 script liner. When the lampshade is completely dry, gently erase the pattern lines with a kneaded eraser.

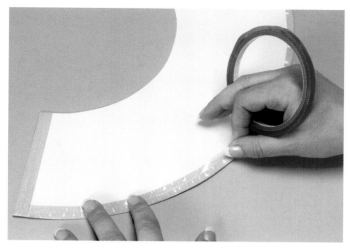

9   ASSEMBLY
Apply two strips of ¼-inch (6mm) Ultra Sticky Craft Tape, side by side, on the inside of the shade along the "*fiore bello*" end. Cut the tape with a craft knife as shown.

10   Apply ¼-inch (6mm) Ultra Sticky Craft Tape along the lower edge on the inside of the shade. Gently ease the tape to adapt to the curve. In the same manner, apply a second strip just above the first. I have used two strips of ¼-inch (6mm) tape because the narrow width will adjust to the curve of the lampshade more readily than a single strip of ½-inch (13mm) tape.

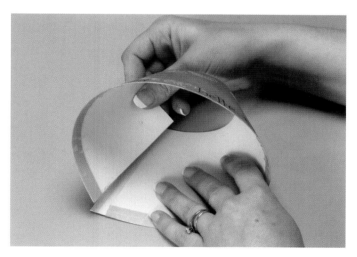

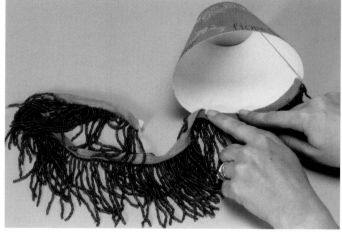

11   Remove the protective top layer from the tape applied in step 9. Curve the shade until the exposed tape overlaps the other end of the shade by ½" (13mm). Press the ends firmly together.

12   Remove the protective top layer from the tape applied in step 10. Firmly press the beaded fringe onto the exposed tape. Cut away excess fringe with scissors or a craft knife. Although working within the curve of the lampshade may seem awkward, attaching the beads at this point helps ensure that the beaded fringe will conform to the curve without puckering.

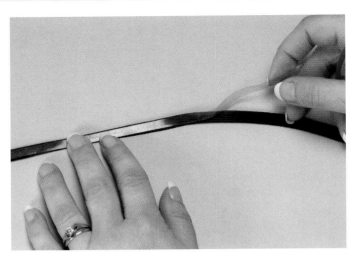

13 Trim the lower edge of the shade with narrow trim. Cut a strip of ¼-inch (6mm) Ultra Sticky Craft Tape down to fit the width of the trim, if necessary, and apply the tape to the back of the trim. Then remove the protective top layer from the tape and, starting at the lampshade seam, press the trim onto the shade. Cut away excess trim with scissors or a craft knife.

14 Apply a strip of ¼" (6mm) Ultra Sticky Craft Tape to the wrong side of the single-fold bias tape.

15 Remove the protective top layer from the tape and apply the bias along the upper edge of the shade. Begin at the seam and attach the bias to the outside of the lampshade, extending approximately ⅛" (3mm) above the top of the shade.

16 Fold the excess width over the edge of the shade and press in place on the inside.

17 The shade can be used as a cover by simply slipping it over an existing shade.

LAMP WITH PORTUGUESE PHRASE SHOWING

FRENCH

ITALIAN

"WELCOME"

Adapting Text to Flow on a Banner

Your guests will feel embraced by the warmth of your home when they are greeted by this lovely welcome banner painted on the wall. The flowing ribbon, enhanced with distinctive lettering that creates the word "welcome," becomes an even greater focal point if surrounded by an "empty" frame that allows the banner's ends to extend beyond the frame's boundaries. The design can be painted on any color wall, which then becomes the background color for the ribbon. For optimum results when working on an alternative background color, replace the Americana colors used to slip-slap the background (Antique White and Sand) with similar-value Americana hues in the same color family as your chosen wall color.

colors and materials

PAINT: DecoArt Americana Acrylics

| Antique White | Sand | Raw Sienna | Traditional Raw Sienna | Traditional Burnt Umber | Dried Basil Green | Plum | Dried Basil Green + Raw Sienna (2:1) |

SURFACE
Interior wall

LOEW-CORNELL BRUSHES
- Mixtique angular, series 8400, ³/₄-inch (19mm)
- Mixtique lettering, series 8100, ¹/₂-inch (13mm)
- Mixtique script liner, series 8050, no. 0
- American Painter bristle fan, series 2200, no. 4
- Crescent, series 247, ¹/₂-inch (13mm)

ADDITIONAL SUPPLIES
- Latex interior wall paint (optional–see project introduction and page 53, step 1)
- Basic supplies (See page 13.)
- Soapstone pencil
- Lint-free cloth
- Water soluble blue transfer paper (chacopaper)

For font identification and help in finding supplies, see Resources on page 126.

PATTERN
This pattern may be hand-traced or photocopied for
personal use only. Enlarge at 111 percent to bring
up to full size.

©2002 Rebecca Baer CDA

SURFACE PREPARATION
1 To replicate the wall color shown, paint the wall with latex interior paint in the brand of your choice, mixed to match DecoArt Americana Antique White. Allow the paint to dry overnight. From this point forward, all paints used are DecoArt Americana paints. As noted in the introduction, you can choose a color other than Antique White for your wall, if desired.

Determine the approximate placement for the ribbon banner and mark lightly with a soapstone pencil, if necessary. You will lose this marking when you dampen the wall. It's only intended to temporarily indicate placement. Read through the remaining steps of the background procedure so that you are familiar with the process. The technique must be executed quickly while the surface remains wet.

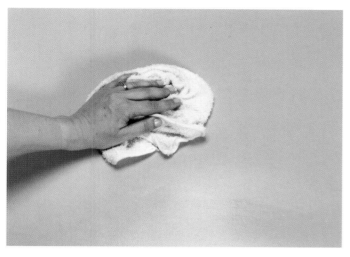

2 Dampen the wall to extend your working time by wiping lightly with a wet, lint-free cloth. The wall should glisten without runs or drips.

3 BACKGROUND
Place separate puddles of Antique White and Sand on your palette. Using a ³⁄₄-inch (19mm) angular, begin slip-slapping the wall with Sand in the general area of the ribbon.

4 Pick up Antique White as you work outward to merge the mottled area with the base color on the wall. Carry the transition well beyond the banner to avoid losing all variation beneath the pattern.

5 As the mottled area dries, the Antique White will darken slightly, becoming a close match with the latex wall paint.

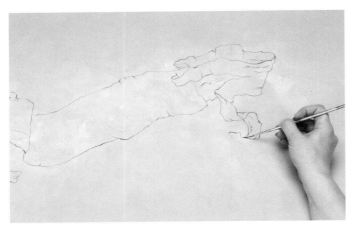

6 | **PAINTING THE BANNER**
When the background treatment is dry, transfer the pattern using water-soluble blue chacopaper and your stylus. Establish a broken outline to the banner using a brush mix of Traditional Raw Sienna + a touch of Traditional Burnt Umber to darken. Thin the paint to an ink-like consistency and apply with a no. 0 script liner. In the same manner, establish detail lines and folds.

7 | Paint the lettering on the banner with slightly thinned Dried Basil Green + Raw Sienna 2:1 on a ½-inch (13mm) lettering brush.

8 | Load a ½-inch (13mm) dry crescent brush with Sand and wipe the brush on a dry paper towel to remove excess paint. Drybrush to create light areas on the banner. Skim the brush across the banner to create texture in other areas as needed.

9 | Using Traditional Raw Sienna + a touch of Traditional Burnt Umber side loaded on a ¾-inch (19mm) angular, wash shading on the banner, walking the color out as necessary. Do not be concerned about creating smooth shading. Irregularities will create added interest and facilitate an aged appearance.

10 | Deepen the shading with additional floats as needed to shape the banner. Vary the proportions of the shading mixture for variety.

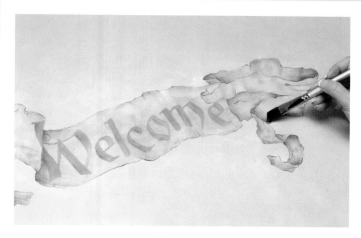

11 | Using a side-loaded ³/₄-inch (19mm) angular, wash the banner with accents of Plum.

12 | Spatter the banner and surrounding area with Plum + a touch of Traditional Burnt Umber on a no. 4 stiff bristle fan, as explained on page 17.

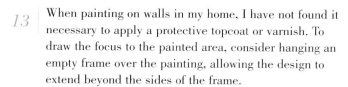

13 | When painting on walls in my home, I have not found it necessary to apply a protective topcoat or varnish. To draw the focus to the painted area, consider hanging an empty frame over the painting, allowing the design to extend beyond the sides of the frame.

Remembered Joys
are never past

PHOTO MAT
Lettering With Paper Crafts

"Remembered joys are never past."

The possible variations of this elegantly lettered and simply stenciled piece are countless—and it's versatility will amaze you. Frame the finished surface and you have an exceptional home for your favorite photo. Or adjust the design to create an entire 12" × 12" (30.5cm x 30.5cm) scrapbook page that gives you space for several photos plus that all-important journaling. A pattern and a color-and-paper list for just such a variation are on pages 64-65. Regardless of your approach, the design and phrase, "Remembered joys are never past," are sure to bring a smile to everyone who views them.

colors and papers

PAINT: DecoArt Americana Acrylics

| Dried Basil Green | Black Plum | Driftwood | Warm Neutral | French Vanilla | Charcoal Grey | Rookwood Red | Black Plum + Dried Basil Green + Charcoal Grey (2:1:1) | Rookwood Red + Driftwood (1:1) |

Mi-Teintes art paper by Canson

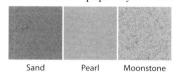

| Sand | Pearl | Moonstone |

Card stock by Paper Garden

Sandblast

MATERIALS ON THE NEXT PAGE

materials

LOEW-CORNELL BRUSHES
- Liner, series 8350, no. 0
- Stencil brush, series 1150, ¾-inch (19mm)

ADDITIONAL SUPPLIES
- Basic supplies (See page 13.)
- Low-tack tape
- Creative Memories custom cutting system (circle patterns; cutting mat with printed gridlines; red, green and blue blades)
- Stencil ST-102 Strokework Background, Simply Elegant Stencils from Rebecca Baer, Inc.
- Antibacterial hand gel
- Soapstone or chalk pencil
- Metal ruler
- Craft knife
- Two-sided tape or sticky squares
- White transfer paper
- Kneaded eraser

For font identification and help in finding supplies, see Resources on page 126.

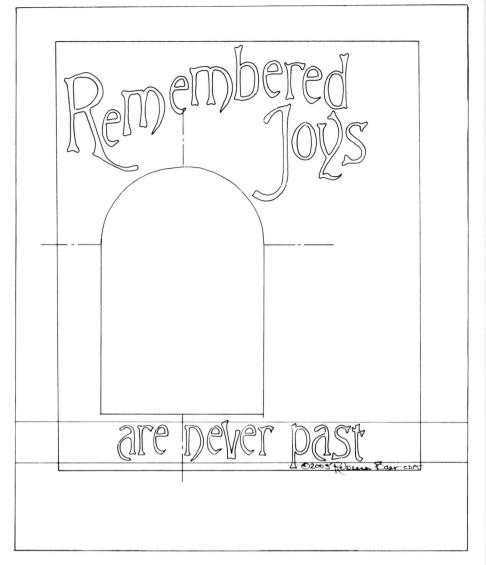

PATTERN
This pattern may be hand-traced or photocopied for personal use only. Enlarge at 170 percent to bring up to full size.

1 STENCILING

Using low-tack tape, secure a sheet of Pearl-colored paper to the cutting mat. I prefer to line up the straight edges of the paper with the cutting grid so that it is not necessary to reposition the paper for subsequent steps. Position Strokework stencil ST-102 over the paper and secure with low-tack tape. Load a ³⁄₄-inch (19mm) stencil brush with Driftwood. Wipe the brush on a paper towel to remove excess paint. Too much paint remaining on the brush will allow the paint to bleed under the stencil. Hold the brush perpendicular to the surface and pounce over the stencil until the strokework is filled in.

2 Using the same stencil brush, rouge (add a hint of color to) small areas of the strokework. Pick up a touch of Warm Neutral on the dirty brush and wipe to remove excess paint. Pounce over random, irregular areas of strokework. When you're satisfied with the stenciling, wash the stencil. Due to its intricate detail, this cleaning must be done carefully. Refer to the instructions under "Stencil Cleaners" on page 11.

3 Pick up a generous amount of French Vanilla on the dirty brush and wipe the brush thoroughly on a paper towel to clear the previous colors. Reload the brush with French Vanilla, wipe off the excess, and rouge small areas of strokework as directed in step 2. With the same brush, pick up Dried Basil Green, wipe off the excess and rouge small areas of strokework. Before removing the stencil, lift the corner to see if there is a noticeable but not abrupt color variation throughout the stenciled area. If you don't notice enough of a difference, strengthen selected areas with the desired color. To correct abrupt color changes, blend the two closest colors on the brush and soften the offending area.

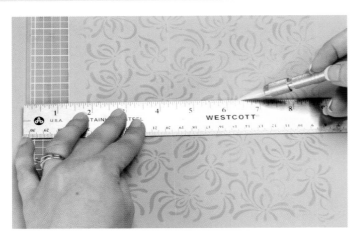

4 ARCHED WINDOW
For the sake of accuracy, always measure and mark cutting lines rather than tracing and transferring from the pattern. Refer to the pattern to determine placement and, using a soapstone pencil and a ruler, measure and mark the centerlines for the circle that will create the arch at the top of the window.

5 Position a circle-cutting template on the centerlines and cut the top half of a 3-inch (7.6cm) diameter circle that begins and ends at the horizontal centerline.

6 Refer to the pattern to determine the desired height of the arched opening. Use a ruler and soapstone pencil to establish the bottom of the arched opening. Cut the sides of the opening, using a metal straightedge and a craft knife.

7 In the same manner, cut the bottom line of the arched opening and then lift out the arched shape.

8 Using the pattern as a guide, use a metal straightedge and a craft knife to trim your stenciled paper to the size of the inner rectangle. As you cut, you may need to add low-tack tape to keep the paper from shifting on the cutting mat.

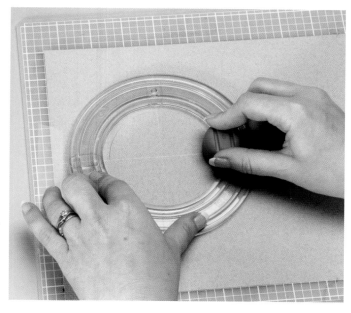

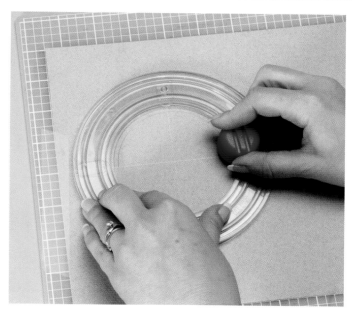

9 EMBELLISHMENTS
On the Moonstone paper, measure and mark centerlines for the circle that will create the top of the arch trim. Make the vertical line 3" (7.6cm) from the left edge of the paper and the horizontal line 4½" (11.4cm) from the bottom of the paper. This allows enough room to cut the entire arched window trim without running off the paper. Then position a 3½-inch (8.9cm) circle pattern on the centerlines and cut the top half of a circle that begins and ends at the horizontal centerline.

10 In the same manner, cut a second half-circle, using a 3¼-inch (8.3cm) circle pattern. If using the cutting system shown, take care not to shift the circle pattern after the first cut. The pattern for cutting these two sizes is the same. Simply cut each half-circle with a different cutting blade, as shown.

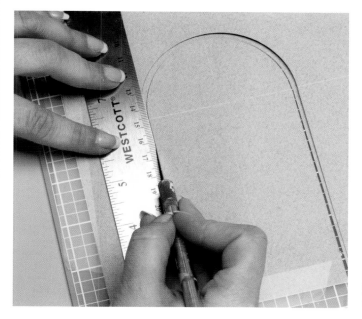

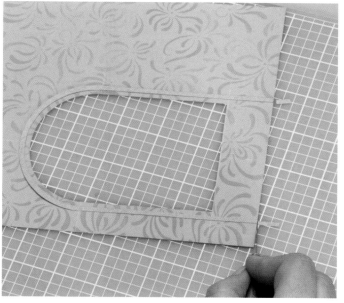

11 Using a metal straightedge and a craft knife, extend the cuts to the bottom of the paper.

12 Use two-sided tape or sticky squares to attach the arched window trim to your stenciled paper. The space between the trim and the arched opening should be about the width of the trim. Cut off the excess trim.

13   Using a metal straightedge and a craft knife, cut a ³⁄₄" × 8" (1.9cm × 20.3cm) strip from the Sand-colored paper. Then cut a 5⅝" × 8" (14.3cm × 20.3cm) rectangle from the same color paper. Center the stenciled paper on the large Sand-colored rectangle and attach with two-sided tape or sticky squares. Be sure you leave a space at the top or side to slip in a photo. (I have temporarily slipped a piece of vellum into the photo space.)

14   Cut an 8" × 10" (20.3cm × 25.4cm) rectangle from your Sandblast card stock. Using your pattern as a guide, position your stenciled and sand-colored composite on the large Sandblast rectangle and attach with two-sided tape or sticky squares. Using the pattern as a guide, position the ³⁄₄" × 8" (1.9cm × 20.3cm) strip on the stenciled paper and attach it in the same manner.

15   **LETTERING**
Transfer the lettering with white transfer paper and a stylus. Using a no. 0 liner, apply the lettering with Black Plum + Dried Basil Green + Charcoal Grey (2:1:1).

16   For a simpler version the lettering can remain as is, or you can detail each letter with an outline of Rookwood Red+ Driftwood (1:1), as shown. Thin the mixture to an ink-like consistency and apply with a no. 0 liner.

17   Erase any remaining pattern lines with a kneaded eraser.

Remembered Joys

are never past

© 2003 Rebecca Baer CDA

SCRAPBOOK-PAGE VARIATION

Use the pattern below and the papers and paint colors indicated on this and the next page to create a totally different look, appropriate for a 12" × 12" (30.5cm × 30.5cm) scrapbook page.

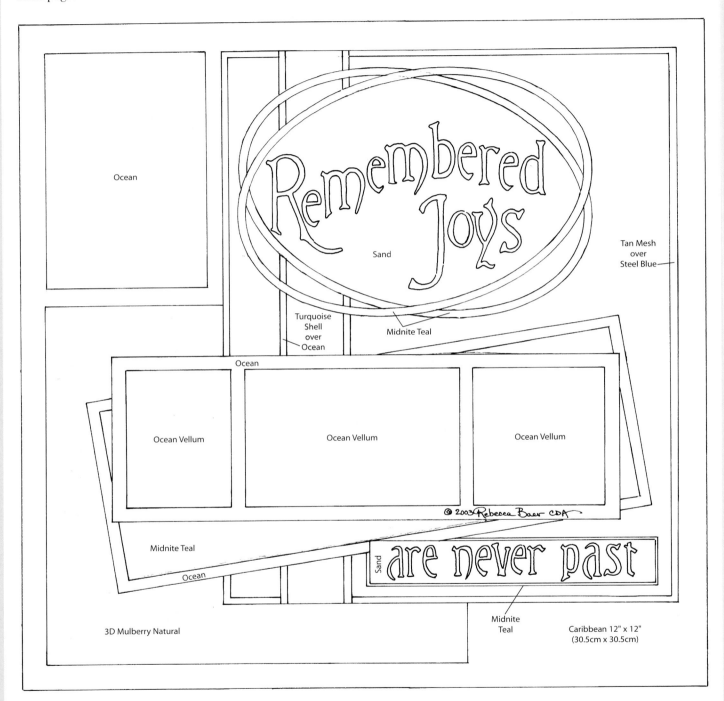

LAYOUT PATTERN

This pattern may be hand-traced or photocopied for personal use only. Enlarge at 167 percent to bring up to full size.

DecoArt Americana Acrylics

Colonial Green
(lettering)

Black Plum
(lettering shadow)

Ice Blue
(spattering of
lettered paper)

Cardstock & Vellum by Paper Garden

Midnite Teal
8½" x 11"
(21.6cm x 27.9cm)
or 12" x12"
(30.5cm x 30.5cm)

Steel Blue
8½" x 11"
(21.6cm x 27.9cm)
or 12" x12"
(30.5cm x 30.5cm)

Ocean
8½" x 11"
(21.6cm x 27.9cm)
or 12" x12"
(30.5cm x 30.5cm)

Mi-Teintes art paper by Canson

Sand

Specialty Paper by Sanook

3D Mulberry Natural
(I used the back,
which has a less
defined pattern.)

Specialty Paper by Creative Imagination

Tan Mesh

Caribbean
12" x12"
(30.5cm x 30.5cm)

Ocean Vellum
8½" x 11"
(21.6cm x 27.9cm)

Turquoise Shell
8½" x 11"
(21.6cm x 27.9cm)

GARDEN SLATE
Lettering For Your Landscape

"All things grow with love."

S late is a perfect surface for projects that will be displayed outside. It's easy to paint on and, as a natural material, blends well with the great outdoors. Applying exterior varnish over painted lettering makes this attractive project practical for outdoor display. It will welcome visitors to explore your garden or just to sit on your patio and enjoy their surroundings. Using the distinctive lettering shown, you can paint the quote I used or your favorite quote or one of the several alternates listed on page 68. Whatever your choice, this garden slate is sure to dress up your landscape.

colors

PAINT: DecoArt Americana Acrylics

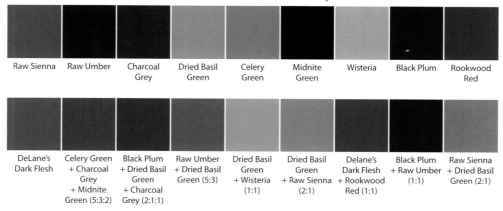

Raw Sienna	Raw Umber	Charcoal Grey	Dried Basil Green	Celery Green	Midnite Green	Wisteria	Black Plum	Rookwood Red
DeLane's Dark Flesh	Celery Green + Charcoal Grey + Midnite Green (5:3:2)	Black Plum + Dried Basil Green + Charcoal Grey (2:1:1)	Raw Umber + Dried Basil Green (5:3)	Dried Basil Green + Wisteria (1:1)	Dried Basil Green + Raw Sienna (2:1)	Delane's Dark Flesh + Rookwood Red (1:1)	Black Plum + Raw Umber (1:1)	Raw Sienna + Dried Basil Green (2:1)

MATERIALS ON THE NEXT PAGE

materials

SURFACE
* Roof slate, available from auctions, flea markets, roofing supply retailers and general craft retailers. I painted this project on a 25" × 10" (63.5cm × 25.4cm) slate, but any size will do. See "Tracing, Enlarging and Reducing the Pattern" on page 14.

LOEW-CORNELL BRUSHES
* Mixtique angular, series 8400
  * ⅛-inch (3mm)
  * ½-inch (13mm)
* Mixtique liner, series 8350, no. 4
* Mixtique script liner, series 8050, no. 0
* Mixtique one stroke lettering, series 8100
  * ¼-inch (6mm)
  * ½-inch (13mm)
* Stencil, series 1150, 1-inch (25mm)

ADDITIONAL SUPPLIES
* Basic supplies (See page 13.)
* Ruler
* Soapstone pencil
* Stencil ST-106 Lattice & Vines Simply Elegant Stencils from Rebecca Baer, Inc.
* Low-tack tape
* Antibacterial hand gel
* White transfer paper
* Kneaded eraser
* Leather lacing
* Varnish (See page 72, step 19.)

For font identification and help in finding supplies, see Resources on page 126.

alternate quotes

The earth laughs in flowers.
RALPH WALDO EMERSON

To everything there is a season.
ECCLESIASTES 3:1

Value the smallest flower as a special favor.
ANONYMOUS

One touch of nature makes the whole world kin.
WILLIAM SHAKESPEARE

PATTERN
This pattern may be hand-traced or photocopied for personal use only. For a 25" × 10" (63.5cm × 25.4cm) slate, enlarge at 200 percent to bring up to full size.

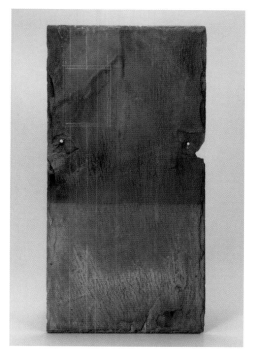

2
Using a ½-inch (13mm)
lettering brush, paint the
vertical band with Celery
Green + Charcoal Grey +
Midnite Green (5:3:2).
Allow occasional skips in
coverage as created by
the textured surface.
Apply a single coat of
Black Plum + Dried
Basil Green + Charcoal
Grey (2:1:1) to the area
within the box. Thin the
paint only slightly and
apply with a ½-inch
(13mm) lettering brush.

1 PRE-STENCILING

Trace the pattern onto tracing paper
and set aside. Make sure the slate is
clean, dry and free of any residue.
For the sake of accuracy, use a ruler
and soapstone pencil to measure and
mark the vertical band and the box
surrounding "All."

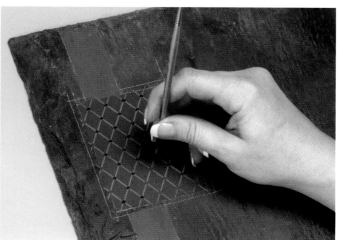

3 STENCILING

Mask the panel and position the large lattice panel from
stencil ST-106 Lattice & Vines within the masked area.
Secure with tape. Pick up Raw Umber + Dried Basil
Green (5:3) on a dry 1-inch (25mm) stencil brush. Wipe
the brush on a paper towel to remove excess paint. Holding the brush perpendicular to the surface, pounce over
the stencil until the lattice is filled in. Due to its intricate detail, the stencil must be cleaned carefully. Refer
to the instructions under "Stencil Cleaners" on page 11.

4 Using the back end of a thin-handled brush, dot each
intersection of the lattice with Black Plum.

5 | **BORDER**
Paint the border surrounding the box with Charcoal Grey on a no. 4 liner. Using a no. 0 script liner, apply a fine line of Black Plum along the inside edge of the Charcoal Grey border. Using a no. 0 script liner, trim both sides of the vertical band with Charcoal Grey.

6 | **LETTERING**
Transfer the pattern for the lettering with white transfer paper and your stylus. Using a ¼-inch (6mm) lettering brush, apply the main body of the letters using Dried Basil Green + Wisteria (1:1).

7 | Switch to a no. 4 liner to paint the rounded ends and extended curves as needed.

8 | Side load a ½-inch (13mm) angular with Dried Basil Green + Raw Sienna (2:1). Begin at the top and walk the color downward so that it diminishes one-half to two-thirds of the way down on each letter.

9 | Using a no. 0 script liner, outline each letter with a fine line of Raw Umber + Dried Basil Green (5:3).

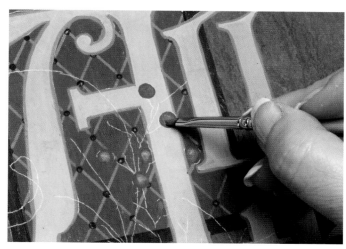

10 **BERRIES**
Transfer the remaining pattern to the slate. Using a ⅛-inch (3mm) angular, apply a single coat of DeLane's Dark Flesh + Rookwood Red (1:1) to the berries.

11 Daub a light area in the upper right quadrant with Delane's Dark Flesh on a ⅛-inch (3mm) angular. Build the lighter berries with the addition of Wisteria on the dirty brush.

12 Daub the strongest lights on selected berries with additional Wisteria.

13 Float the lower left of each berry with Black Plum on a ⅛-inch (3mm) angular.

14 Daub the blossom end, as seen on the patterns, with thin Dried Basil Green + Raw Sienna (2:1) on a no. 0 script liner.

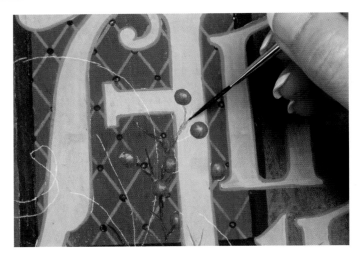

15 | BRANCHES
Thin Black Plum + Raw Umber (1:1) to wash consistency and, using a no. 0 script liner, apply in an irregular manner to create branches with texture.

16 | With the same brush, apply highlights with broken, thin lines of Dried Basil Green + Raw Sienna (2:1) thinned to an ink-like consistency.

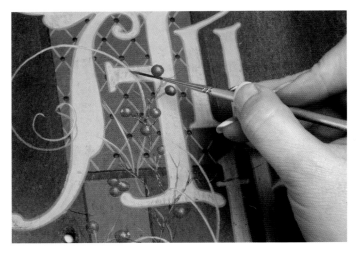

17 | TENDRILS
Using a no. 0 script liner, establish the tendrils with Raw Sienna + Dried Basil Green (2:1) thinned to an ink-like consistency. Build light areas on portions of the tendrils that you wish to bring forward by first adding a touch of Dried Basil Green to the dirty brush and painting over these segments. Further lighten the paint with additional Dried Basil Green on the brush and paint a shorter segment within the previous application. For the lightest areas, add a touch of Wisteria to the dirty brush and place a small highlight on the most forward portion. See "Building a Thin-line Highlight," page 17, for a closer view of this technique. Wash over the tendrils with thin Raw Sienna.

18 | FINISHING
Remove remaining pattern lines with a kneaded eraser. To hang the slate, cut an appropriate length of leather lacing and pass the ends through the slate's holes from the back. Tie each end in a double knot to keep it from sliding back through the hole. Trim the ends.

19 | The finished slate can be displayed indoors without varnish. For outdoor use, choose an exterior varnish in your favorite sheen. Slate is porous and should be finished on both front and back for complete protection.

All things grow with Love

©2003
Rebecca Baer CDA

BUTTER CROCKS

Painting Custom Labels

The crocks used for this project are glazed on the inside, making them food safe. To protect and preserve the painting on the outside of the crocks, clean them by wiping with a damp cloth and never immerse them in water. For this reason, I prefer to place any food items in a second container that fits inside the crock. If you use an insert that is more shallow than the crock, there will be enough room for a layer of crushed ice under the insert, enabling you to keep the contents chilled during use.

Whether you choose to serve a homemade flavored spread like those described on page 85 or a purchased one, you can be sure it will not only taste great, but will also look fantastic in these painted crocks.

colors

PAINT: DecoArt Americana Acrylics

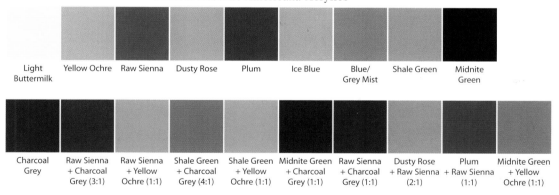

Light Buttermilk	Yellow Ochre	Raw Sienna	Dusty Rose	Plum	Ice Blue	Blue/ Grey Mist	Shale Green	Midnite Green

Charcoal Grey	Raw Sienna + Charcoal Grey (3:1)	Raw Sienna + Yellow Ochre (1:1)	Shale Green + Charcoal Grey (4:1)	Shale Green + Yellow Ochre (1:1)	Midnite Green + Charcoal Grey (1:1)	Raw Sienna + Charcoal Grey (1:1)	Dusty Rose + Raw Sienna (2:1)	Plum + Raw Sienna (1:1)	Midnite Green + Yellow Ochre (1:1)

MATERIALS ON THE NEXT PAGE

SURFACE

small snap lid canisters
   from The Creative C.A.T.
   4" (10.2cm) diameter and height (not
   including wire handle)

LOEW-CORNELL BRUSHES

- Mixtique angular, series 8400
   - $\frac{1}{8}$-inch (3mm)
   - $\frac{1}{4}$-inch (6mm) Not used on oregano crock
   - $\frac{3}{8}$-inch (10mm) Not used on oregano crock.
   - $\frac{1}{2}$-inch (13mm)
   - $\frac{3}{4}$-inch (19mm)
- Mixtique round, series 8000
   - no. 3/0
   - no. 4
- Mixtique script liner, series 8050, no. 0
- Crescent, series 247
   - $\frac{1}{8}$-inch (3mm) Not used on oregano crock.
   - $\frac{1}{4}$-inch (6mm) Used only on garlic crock.
- Touche, item 38
- Stencil, series 1150, $\frac{1}{2}$-inch (13mm)

ADDITIONAL SUPPLIES

- Basic supplies (See page 13.)
- Fine sanding pad
- DecoArt Multi-Purpose Sealer
- $\frac{1}{2}$-inch (13mm) masking tape
- Stencil ST-102 Strokework Background,
   Simply Elegant Stencils by Rebecca Baer, Inc.
- Antibacterial hand gel
- Measuring tape
- Soapstone or chalk pencil
- Saral white transfer paper (Use a new sheet for
   best visibility.)
- DecoArt Weathered Wood crackling medium
- Kneaded eraser
- Krylon 1311

For font identification and help in finding
supplies, see Resources on page 126.

PATTERN

These patterns may be hand-traced or photocopied for personal use only. Enlarge at
143 percent to bring up to full size.

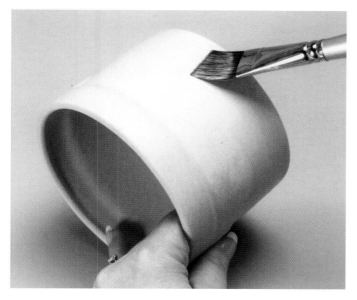

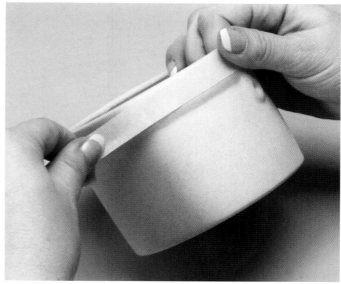

1   **SURFACE PREPARATION**
If the surface is rough, sand lightly and wipe the surface with a damp paper towel to remove sanding dust. Do not use a tack cloth as it may leave an undesirable residue.

    Due to stoneware's porous nature, I find acrylic paint adheres very well without sealer. However, mistakes are easier to remove from sealed stoneware. So if you wish to seal the crocks, apply a single coat of multi-purpose sealer to the exterior.

2   Trace the desired pattern(s) and set them aside. Do not transfer the patterns at this time. Mask off the raised band at the top of each crock with ½-inch (13mm) masking tape.

3   **STENCILING**
Position strokework stencil ST-102 on the crock and secure with tape. Load a ½-inch (13mm) stencil brush with Ice Blue. Wipe the brush on a paper towel to remove excess paint. Too much paint remaining on the brush will allow the paint to bleed under the stencil. Holding the brush perpendicular to the surface, pounce over a series of unconnected, irregular stencil areas, each no larger than 2" (5.1cm) to 3" (7.6cm) in length or height.

4   Pick up Shale Green on the dirty brush and wipe to remove excess. Begin pouncing unpainted areas, overlapping the patches where you last finished. The end result should be a gradual transition between patches of Ice Blue and Shale Green. Do not remove the stencil.

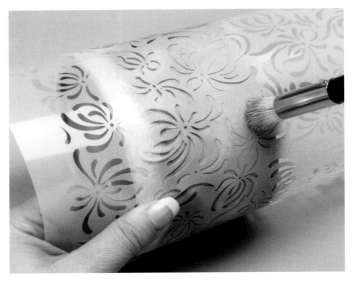

5 | Using a clean ½-inch (13mm) stencil brush, rouge (i.e. add a hint of color to) small areas of strokework with a touch of Dusty Rose. Then blend a hint of Plum into the dirty brush, being careful not to let the color become too strong. Again, rouge small areas. Before removing the stencil, lift the corner to see if there is a noticeable but not abrupt color variation throughout the stenciled area. If you don't notice enough of a difference, strengthen selected areas with the desired color. To correct abrupt color changes, blend the two closest colors on the brush and soften the offending area.

6 | Reposition the stencil as needed and repeat the procedure until the background is completed. You may find it necessary to mask sections where the stencil overlaps previously completed areas. In the same manner, stencil the flat rim on the lid of the crock. Repeat the stenciling process on each crock, reserving one stencil brush for use with Ice Blue and Shale Green and the other for Plum and Dusty Rose to avoid muddying the colors. Due to its intricate detail, the stencil must be cleaned carefully. Refer to the instructions under "Stencil Cleaners" on page 11.

7 | LABEL BACKGROUND AND BORDER
Using a measuring tape, measure between the crock's handle holes and mark the vertical center with a soapstone or chalk pencil.

8 | Using the centerline for guidance, position the pattern on the crock and secure with tape. Transfer the oval outline to each crock, using white transfer paper and a stylus. Basecoat the inner oval with a single thin coat of Charcoal Grey applied with a ½-inch (13mm) angular. Choppy or irregular coverage is not a problem due to additional layers. Apply a few random patches of Weathered Wood crackling medium to the oval with a ½-inch (13mm) angular and allow the surface to dry.

9   Using a ½-inch (13mm) angular, apply a thin layer of Blue/Grey Mist over the Weathered Wood and Charcoal Grey base. Apply with short strokes in varying directions—a slightly choppy look will help to create a vintage appearance. Do not go over any area more than once, or you may shift or lift the crackled areas. Let the surface air dry for cracks to appear.

10   Wash the extensions at the ends of the inner oval with a hint of Raw Sienna + Charcoal Grey (3:1) on a no. 4 round. Using the same brush, trim the inside slope bordering the flat rim of the lid. With the same mixture, trim the perimeter of the lid using a touche.

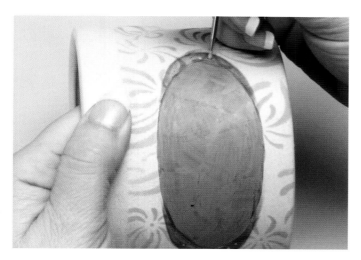

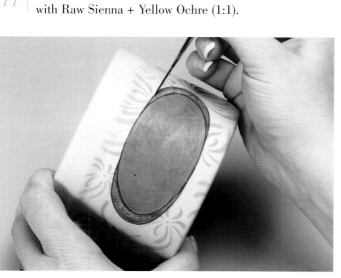

11   Using a stylus, apply descending dots on each extension with Raw Sienna + Yellow Ochre (1:1).

12   Use a kneaded eraser to remove any visible lines from the crock and then mist the exterior with Krylon 1311 to protect the crackle. If you have time to wait, you can allow the crackle to cure for 24 hours and eliminate spraying the surface. Using a ¾-inch (19mm) angular, wash over the inner oval with a hint of Raw Sienna.

13   Using a no. 0 script liner, trim both the inner and outer ovals with a fine line of thinned Charcoal Grey. Transfer the remaining pattern segments to each crock, using white transfer paper and a stylus. Each of the rim designs is repeated to encircle the crock. Refer to the photos on pages 84 and 85 for clarification.

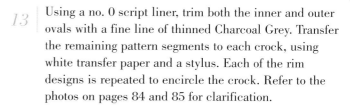

Roasted Garlic and Rosemary Crock

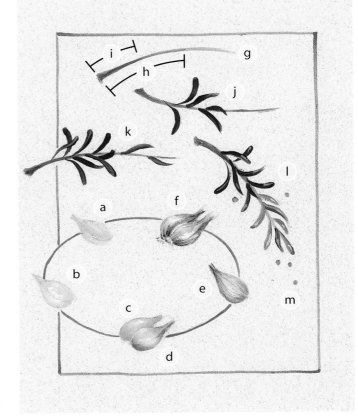

STEP 14: ROASTED GARLIC AND ROSEMARY CROCK

14

GARLIC

a. Using a no. 4 round, apply a single wash-consistency coat of Yellow Ochre to each clove, using lengthwise strokes.

b. Using lengthwise strokes, drybrush highlights with Yellow Ochre + Light Buttermilk on a ¹/₈-inch (3mm) to ¹/₄-inch (6mm) crescent dry brush. Daub the strongest highlights with Light Buttermilk on the tip of a ¹/₈-inch (3mm) angular.

c. Float shading with Dusty Rose + Raw Sienna (2:1). Apply with a side-loaded ¹/₄-inch (6mm) angular.

d. Reinforce the shading in a more narrow area with Plum + Raw Sienna (1:1). Apply with a side-loaded ¹/₈-inch (3mm) angular.

e. Referring to your pattern, apply fine lines with Yellow Ochre + a touch of Light Buttermilk +/-. Thin to linework consistency and apply with a no. 0 script liner. Repeat with very thin Plum + a touch of Charcoal Grey. Keep the lines fluid and natural, varying the placement of the colors.

f. Since the details may have softened the highlight, you will want to strengthen the strongest highlights on the cloves, using Light Buttermilk on the tip of a ¹/₈-inch (3mm) angular. Daub tiny roots on the cloves with Yellow Ochre + a touch of Light Buttermilk +/-. Thin to linework consistency and apply with a no. 0 script liner.

ROSEMARY

g. Establish each stem with Shale Green on a no. 0 script liner.

h. Wash the back two-thirds of each stem with Plum. Gradually lift the brush to end the wash so as not to leave a harsh line of color change. Apply with a no. 0 script liner.

i. Wash the back one-third of each stem with Midnite Green. Gradually lift the brush to end the wash so as not to leave a harsh line of color change. Apply with a no. 0 script liner.

j. Refer to the color worksheet as you apply the individual leaves to the stems. Apply each leaf area with the colors listed, thin slightly and apply with a no. 0 script

liner. Place the following colors and mixtures on your palette: Midnite Green, Plum, Shale Green, and Midnite Green + Yellow Ochre (1:1). Apply the individual leaves with a double-loaded 0 script liner. As a general guideline, begin by using the darker combinations at the base of each stem and progress to lighter values toward the tip. Load the brush with any of the colors listed, lightly tip with another color. I began with Midnite Green tipped with Plum.

k. Continue to fill in the leaves using Midnite Green tipped with Shale Green and then Shale Green tipped with Midnite Green + Yellow Ochre (1:1). Allow variety in the double-loaded values to keep all of the leaves from looking the same.

l. Refer to the color worksheet and daub highlights of Yellow Ochre (or Light Buttermilk for the lightest leaves) to the individual leaves. The highlights should become softer as you move into the areas of darker leaves. Apply with a no. 0 script liner.

m. Using a stylus, apply dots mingled among the rosemary with Dusty Rose + Raw Sienna (2:1). See page 83 for lettering instructions.

Greek Oregano Crock

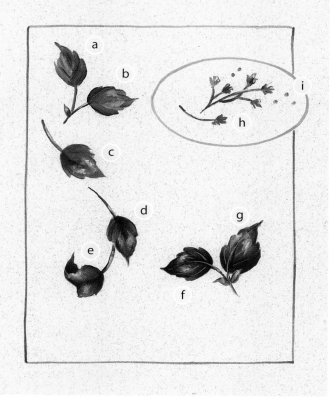

STEP 15: GREEK OREGANO CROCK

15

LEAVES AND STEMS

a. Load a no. 3/0 round with slightly thinned Midnite Green. Tip into Shale Green and blend slightly, allowing the paint to remain streaky. Fill in each leaf with shape-following strokes in a direction consistent with side vein lines. You should be able to fill in each leaf with just a few strokes on each side. Apply the smallest leaves with a single stroke. Apply the stems using a no. 0 script liner double loaded with thin Midnite Green and thin Shale Green.

b. With the tip of a ⅛-inch (3mm) angular side loaded with Yellow Ochre, daub highlights on each leaf. Reinforce highlights on selected leaves with a small daub of Light Buttermilk placed within the Yellow Ochre. Apply highlights to the stems using a no. 0 script liner.

c. Apply a float of thin Plum along the outside curve of the center vein with a ⅛-inch (3mm) angular. Float the back end of each leaf with the same.

d. Deepen the shading slightly with a more narrow float of very thin Midnite Green along the outside curve of the center vein with a ⅛-inch (3mm) angular. Reinforce the shading on the back end of each leaf and float the tip of each leaf with the same. Shade the lower side of the stems with very thin Midnite Green on a no. 0 script liner. Because the tiniest leaves have some variation in value from being applied with a double-loaded brush, it is not necessary to do anything further to those.

e. Apply Charcoal Grey in triangular-shaped dark areas. Apply with a ⅛-inch (3mm) angular. You will find these areas primarily where a leaf is overlapped. Wash selected leaves with a hint of Raw Sienna in the light areas to help create variety among the leaves.

f. Thin Shale Green + Yellow Ochre as needed for visibility to linework consistency. Apply the center and side veins with a no. 0 script liner.

g. Wash over the stems with transparent Plum on a no. 0 script liner.

BLOSSOMS

h. Double load a no. 3/0 round with Dusty Rose and Plum. With short strokes, establish tiny blossoms on the oregano as shown on the pattern. Angle the sides of each blossom outward and the center straight ahead to resemble a tiny fan. Daub tiny highlights with Light Buttermilk on a no. 3/0 round.

i. Using a stylus, apply dots mingled among the oregano with Raw Sienna + Yellow Ochre (1:1). See page 83 for lettering instructions.

Honey Butter Crock

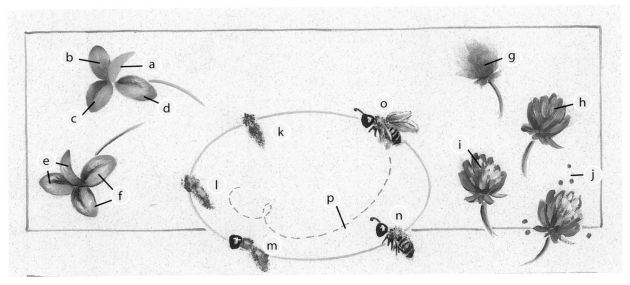

STEP 16: HONEY BUTTER CROCK

16

CLOVER

a. Apply a single, thin coat of Shale Green to each leaf with a no. 3/0 round. The leaves will fill in with only one or two strokes. Add the stems with the same color, using a no. 0 script liner.

b. Float shading in a crescent shape at the base and tip of each leaf, with Shale Green + Charcoal Grey (4:1) on a ⅜-inch (10mm) to ¼-inch (6mm) angular, depending on the size of the leaf.

c. Float against the outside curve of the center vein of each leaf with very thin Midnite Green on a ¼-inch (6mm) to ⅛-inch (3mm) angular.

d. With a no. 0 script liner, apply short detail lines as shown on the pattern, using Shale Green + Yellow Ochre (1:1).

e. Daub a small highlight on each leaf with thin Light Buttermilk on the tip of a no. 0 script liner.

f. Create a fine center vein line using very thin Midnite Green + Charcoal Grey (1:1). Apply with a no. 0 script liner. Using the same brush, apply a loose, broken outline to define the leaves and indicate a shadow on the lower side of the stems.

BLOSSOMS

g. Using a side-loaded ⅜-inch (10mm) angular, apply a thin coat of Plum to each blossom. Keep the paint side of the brush toward the center and walk the water side of the brush around so the color fades at the outer edge.

h. Place the following colors on your palette: Plum, Dusty Rose and Light Buttermilk. Load the brush with any of the colors listed and lightly tip with another color. I began with Plum tipped with Dusty Rose. Apply short strokes with a double-loaded no. 3/0 round.

i. Continue to layer strokes as you progress through Dusty Rose and Light Buttermilk including all brush mixed values between. Allow variety in the double-loaded values to keep all of the strokes from looking the same. Tap several highlights on the blossoms using Light Buttermilk on a no. 3/0 round.

j. Using a stylus, apply dots mingled among the clover with Raw Sienna + Yellow Ochre (1:1).

HONEY BEE

k. Lightly tap in the body of the bee with Raw Sienna + Charcoal Grey (1:1), using a ⅛-inch (3mm) crescent dry brush.

l. Daub light areas along the upper side with Raw Sienna + Yellow Ochre (1:1) on a ⅛-inch (3mm) crescent dry brush.

m. Add the head to the bee with Charcoal Grey on a no. 3/0 round. Highlight with a speck of Light Buttermilk.

n. Detail the bee with very thin Charcoal Grey on a no. 0 script liner. These areas include the antennae, legs and body stripes.

o. Apply the wings to the bee with a wash of very thin Charcoal Grey on a no. 3/0 round and highlight the wings with thin streaks of Light Buttermilk on a no. 0 script liner.

p. Create the dotted flight trail with very thin Raw Sienna + Charcoal Grey (1:1) on a no. 0 script liner.

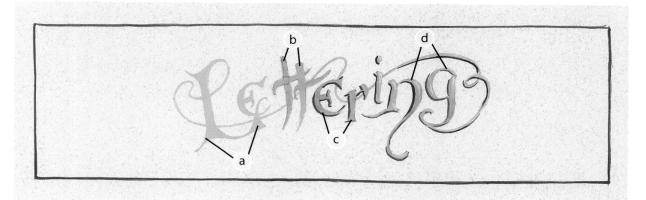

STEP 17: LETTERING

17 | LETTERING FOR ALL CROCKS

a. Apply the lettering on each label with Yellow Ochre. Flatten a no. 3/0 round as you load it in order to create the thick and thin areas (the same way you would use a calligraphy pen) as you apply the lettering on each label with Yellow Ochre. Use a no. 0 script liner to create the thin extensions on selected letters.

b. Wash each letter with Charcoal Grey on a no. 3/0 round.

c. Shade each letter on the lower left with a fine line of Charcoal Grey on a no. 0 script liner.

d. Using a no. 0 script liner, streak small highlights of Yellow Ochre toward the upper right of each letter.

lettering TIP

Don't be concerned about minor irregularities in your lettering; they will enhance the labels' vintage look.

ROASTED GARLIC AND ROSEMARY CROCK: FRONT

GREEK OREGANO CROCK: FRONT

HONEY BUTTER CROCK: FRONT

HONEY BUTTER CROCK: BACK

ROASTED GARLIC AND ROSEMARY CROCK: BACK RIM

GREEK OREGANO CROCK: BACK RIM

CROCK LID

Creating Your Own Flavored Spreads

To create your own flavored spreads, begin with a stick of real butter that has been allowed to sit at room temperature until it is soft. Place the butter and 1 to 2 tablespoons of chopped fresh herbs in a bowl and combine with a fork. If you prefer whipped butter, combine the ingredients using an electric mixer until they are light and fluffy. If you are using dried herbs, you will need only 1 to 2 teaspoons to flavor the butter since dried herbs have a more intense flavor than fresh herbs.

You are limited only by your imagination—choose from an assortment of herbs or fruits, used alone or in combination. In addition, a tablespoon or two of honey gives a marvelous flavor to butter. Honey is available in many varieties, and can be combined with spices such as cinnamon. For a really special treat, mix chopped pecans into the butter once the honey has been incorporated. Adjust the quantity of herbs or other flavorings to suit your taste. If you prefer, cream cheese can be substituted for butter.

RECIPE BOX

Lettering with Other Design Elements

The warm brown eggs and antique eggbeater design on this unique recipe box will bring back vivid memories of your grandmother's kitchen. You can almost smell the aroma of baking sugar cookies. The soft green background with deep green trim plus the golden stenciled detailing and lettering create a very soft and pleasing effect that looks good in any kitchen, regardless of the décor.

colors

PAINT: DecoArt Americana Acrylics

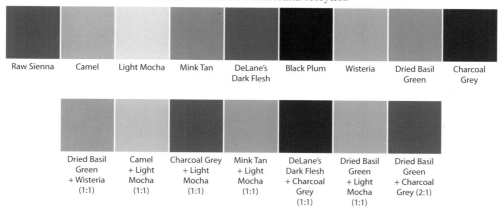

| Raw Sienna | Camel | Light Mocha | Mink Tan | DeLane's Dark Flesh | Black Plum | Wisteria | Dried Basil Green | Charcoal Grey |

| Dried Basil Green + Wisteria (1:1) | Camel + Light Mocha (1:1) | Charcoal Grey + Light Mocha (1:1) | Mink Tan + Light Mocha (1:1) | DeLane's Dark Flesh + Charcoal Grey (1:1) | Dried Basil Green + Light Mocha (1:1) | Dried Basil Green + Charcoal Grey (2:1) |

MATERIALS ON THE NEXT PAGE

materials

SURFACE
Wall-hanging, pull-down recipe box
item 1453 from Wayne's Woodenware

LOEW-CORNELL BRUSHES
- Mixtique angular, series 8400
  - ¹⁄₈-inch (3mm)
  - ¹⁄₄-inch (6mm)
  - ³⁄₈-inch (10mm)
  - ¹⁄₂-inch (13mm)
  - ³⁄₄-inch (19mm)
- Mixtique round, series 8000, no. 2
- Mixtique script liner, series 8050, no. 0
- Mixtique lettering, series 8100, ¹⁄₈-inch (3mm)
- American Painter bristle fan, series 2200, no. 4
- Crescent, series 247, ³⁄₈-inch (10mm)
- Stencil, series 1150
  - ¹⁄₂-inch (13mm)
  - 1-inch (25mm)

ADDITIONAL SUPPLIES
- Basic supplies (See page 13.)
- J.W. etc.'s Wood Filler
- Fine sanding pad
- Wood sealer of choice
- Petit four sponge or dense foam roller
- Soapstone pencil
- Cork-backed ruler
- Stencil ST-106 Lattice & Vines, Simply Elegant Stencils from Rebecca Baer, Inc.
- ¹⁄₄-inch (6mm) masking tape
- ¹⁄₂-inch (13mm) masking tape
- Antibacterial hand gel
- Loew-Cornell Fine Line Painting Pen (optional)
- White transfer paper
- Varnish (See page 96, step 36.)

For font identification and help in finding
supplies, see Resources on page 126.

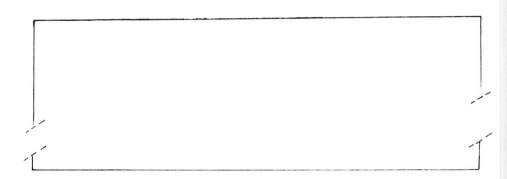

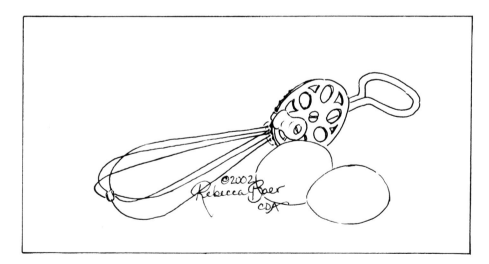

PATTERN
This pattern may be hand-traced or photocopied for personal use only. Enlarge at 118
percent to bring up to full size.

1 SURFACE PREPARATION

Trace the pattern. Do not transfer at this time. Remove the dowel pins in order to separate the door from the box, and fill any dents or nail holes with wood filler. When dry, sand the filler so that the surface is smooth. Seal the box and door, if desired, using your favorite wood sealer. Let dry. Then sand lightly and remove the sanding dust. Using a dense foam roller or petit four sponge, basecoat the exterior of the door and the entire box with Dried Basil Green + Wisteria (1:1). I have opted to allow the card slots to remain natural, but they could be basecoated according to your preference. Using a soapstone pencil and a ruler, measure and mark to establish the panels on the front of the drop-down door as seen on the pattern. Find and mark the vertical centerline on the door (see page 15).

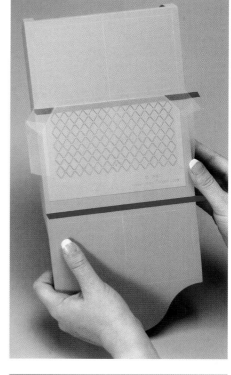

2 STENCILING

Mask the door along the top and bottom of the center section with ¼-inch (6mm) tape. It is not necessary to mask the sides. Using the centerline, position the small lattice panel from stencil ST-106 Lattice & Vines at the top of the masked area. Secure in place with low-tack tape.

3 Pick up Camel on a dry 1-inch (25mm) stencil brush. Wipe the brush on a paper towel to remove excess paint. Holding the brush perpendicular to the surface, pounce over the stencil until the lattice is filled in. Without moving the stencil, pick up Light Mocha on the dirty brush. Wipe to remove excess and pounce random patches of lattice to highlight. Move the stencil down to complete the lattice within the masked area. It is helpful to overlap a full row of lattice to achieve accurate spacing. When the lattice is complete, remove the tape.

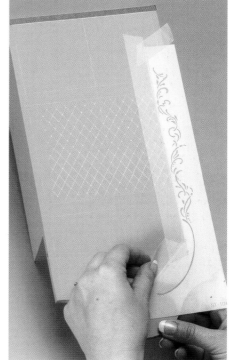

4 Combine Camel + Light Mocha (1:1) and, using your stylus, dot each intersection of the lattice. Then mask off the upper edge of the top panel. With the long curve at the bottom, position the trailing vine from ST-106 approximately ⅛" (3mm) from the outside edge of the door, as shown.

5 | Pick up Raw Sienna on a clean, dry ½-inch (13mm) stencil brush. Wipe the brush on a paper towel to remove excess paint. Holding the brush perpendicular to the surface, pounce over the stencil until the vine is filled in. Without moving the stencil, pick up DeLane's Dark Flesh on the dirty brush. Wipe to remove excess and pounce or swirl gently over random patches of the vine to rouge. Reposition the vine as needed to complete the borders along both edges of the door. In the same manner, apply the scroll to the extensions at the bottom of the door and the top of the box. Refer to the photo on page 97 to see the scrollwork on the box extension.

The remaining areas can be stenciled at any time because they will not interfere with the design areas. Using a soapstone pencil and a ruler, find and mark a vertical centerline on the top and both sides of the recipe box. In the same manner, establish a horizontal centerline. Apply ½-inch (13mm) tape along all four edges to create a panel with a ½-inch (13mm) border on the top and both sides of the recipe box. Using the centerlines, position the large lattice panel from stencil ST-106 "Lattice & Vines" in the center of the masked area. Stencil as described in step 3, repositioning the panel as needed to complete the lattice on the box. Due to its intricate detail, the stencil must be cleaned carefully. Refer to the instructions under "Stencil Cleaners" on page 11.

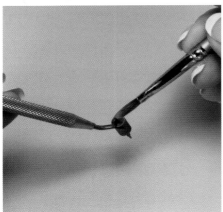

6 | TRIM
Trim all panels on the door and the box with a fine line of Delane's Dark Flesh, breaking the trim line where it meets with the stenciled scrollwork. You can apply the linework trim using either a no. 0 script liner or a fine line painting pen. To use the fine line painting pen, thin the desired color with water so that the paint is an ink-like consistency. Use a round brush to fill the well with the thinned paint as shown.

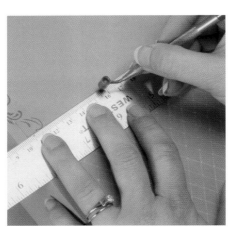

7 | Place a cork-backed ruler in the desired position and hold firmly in place. Tap the loaded pen lightly on your palette before beginning the line to avoid a bead at the starting point. Running the pen along the ruler at a consistent speed, create the line in one continuous motion. Lift off immediately at the end of the line to avoid a bead at the stopping point.

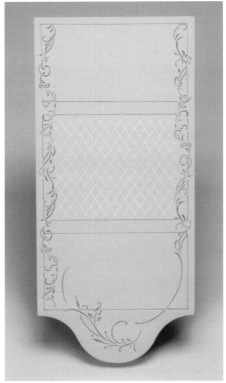

8 | In the same manner, use the painting pen to complete all of the straight lines on the door and box. Clean the painting pen immediately after use to keep the paint from drying and clogging the tip.

9 | **EGGBEATER**
Transfer the pattern to the bottom door panel using white transfer paper and your stylus. Establish the wires on the beater with Charcoal Grey on a no. 0 script liner.

10 | Gradually build light areas on the wires to bring various segments forward. First lighten Charcoal Grey by adding a touch of Light Mocha to the dirty brush. Paint over the portions of the wires you want to bring forward. Then further lighten the mixture with additional Light Mocha and paint a shorter segment within the previous application. In this way you will pyramid progressively lighter values on the wires in ever-shortening lengths. The highlight falls on the curve of the outermost wires. Use Light Mocha to place the final highlight on the outer wires, as shown. See page 17 for a closer view of this technique.

 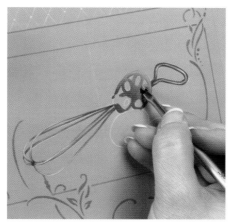 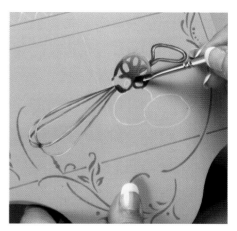

11 | In the same manner, use a no. 2 round to paint and highlight the wire handle of the beater. Build the values with Charcoal Grey + Light Mocha as needed to lighten.

12 | Combine Charcoal Grey + Light Mocha (1:1). Use this medium-gray mixture to base the wheel. Using a ⅛-inch (3mm) angular side loaded with the medium-gray mixture, tip the brush into Light Mocha and blend slightly. Highlight the wheel along the upper right and then carry the light inward by walking the brush between the openings on the wheel toward the lower left, fading at the center.

13 | Using a ⅛-inch (3mm) angular side loaded with the medium-grey mixture, tip the brush into Charcoal Grey and blend slightly. Shade the wheel along the lower left and then carry the shading inward by walking the brush between the openings on the wheel toward the upper right, fading at the center.

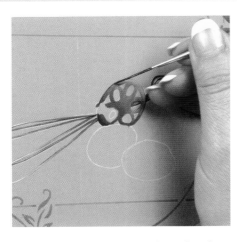

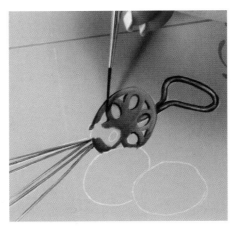

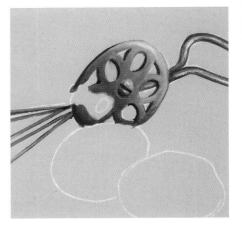

14 Using a no. 0 script liner, brush mix a grey value that is slightly darker than the wheel and apply the thickness of the wheel along the top and left edges.

15 In the same manner, apply thickness to the inside of the wheel openings.

16 Load a ⅛-inch (3mm) angular as described in step 12 and then stroke the upper half of the center screw on the wheel. Using the tip of the brush, daub a highlight of Light Mocha just above the slot. Load a ⅛-inch (3mm) angular as described in step 13, and then stroke the lower half of the center screw on the wheel. Create the slot in the screw using the chisel edge of the brush.

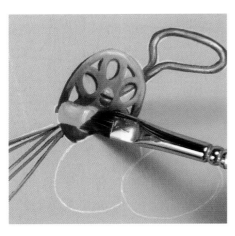

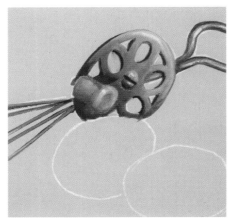

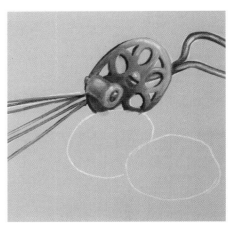

17 Base the wooden knob with Mink Tan. Daub light areas on the knob with Light Mocha on the tip of a ¼-inch (6mm) angular and then wash over the light areas with Raw Sienna.

18 Load a ¼-inch (6mm) angular with Raw Sienna and then pick up a hint of Charcoal Grey on the tip. Blend on the palette for a smooth transition and then float the shading on the knob as shown.

19 Using a ⅛-inch (3mm) angular side loaded with Charcoal Grey + Light Mocha (1:1), apply the metal end on the knob. Using the tip of the brush, daub a highlight of Light Mocha on the upper right. Using a side-loaded ¼-inch (6mm) angular, softly tint the egg-beater with thin Wisteria. Accent with side-loaded Black Plum.

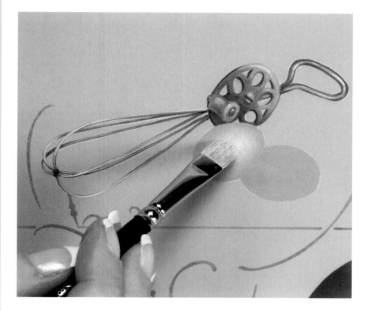

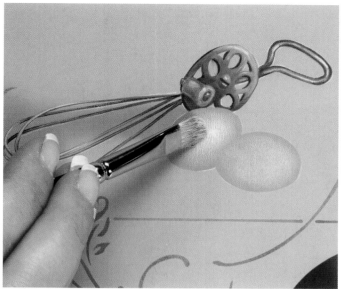

20 EGGS

Using a ³⁄₈-inch (10mm) angular, apply a single coat of Mink Tan to each egg. Fully opaque coverage is not needed due to additional layers over the basecoat. Drybrush highlights with Mink Tan + a touch of Light Mocha on a ³⁄₈-inch (10mm) dry crescent brush. DO NOT WET THE BRUSH. Pick up a small amount of paint on the crescent drybrush. Work the paint into the bristles by wiping the brush across a dry paper towel until there is very little paint coming off the brush. Use the paint remaining in the brush to drybrush the eggs. Apply the paint to the light areas (upper right quadrant) on each egg and walk out using rounded, shape-following strokes.

21 To build the highlight, you will need to drybrush additional Light Mocha in a slightly smaller area within the first application so you have a gradual lightening toward the highlight.

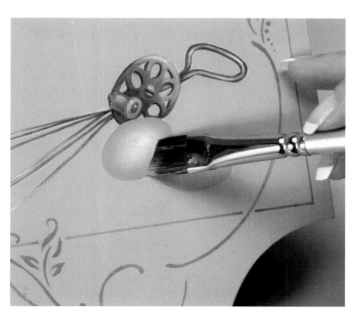

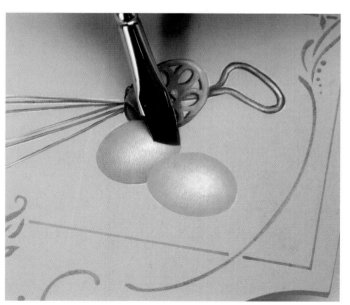

22 Float the edges with Mink Tan + a touch of Raw Sienna on a ¹⁄₂-inch (13mm) angular. Note that the float is widest on the lower left of each egg.

23 Reinforce the shading in a more narrow area with very thin DeLane's Dark Flesh + Charcoal Grey (1:1) on a ³⁄₈-inch (10mm) angular.

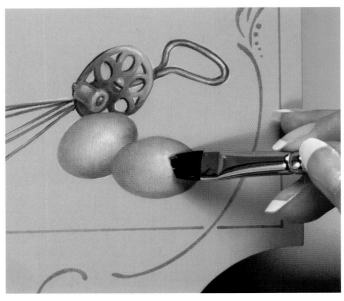

24 | On the back egg, apply additional DeLane's Dark Flesh + Charcoal Grey (1:1) in triangular and crescent-shaped dark areas with a ³⁄₈-inch (10mm) angular.

25 | Daub the final highlight within the light area with Light Mocha side loaded on the tip of a ³⁄₈-inch (10mm) angular.

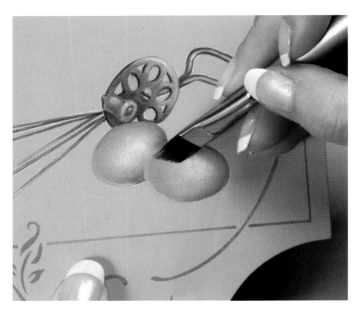

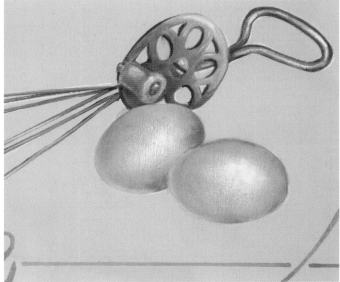

26 | Apply a very narrow float of reflected light along the lower left edge of each egg with Dried Basil Green + Light Mocha (1:1) on the tip of a ³⁄₈-inch (10mm) angular.

27 | Softly tint and accent the eggs by applying thin Wisteria, Black Plum and Raw Sienna one at a time with a side-loaded ³⁄₈-inch (10mm) angular. Place the colors in areas of like value as desired.

28 | LETTERING
Using a ⅛-inch (3mm) lettering brush, thin Mink Tan only as necessary for adequate flow. Paint the word "Recipe" in the upper panel, applying light pressure to the brush so the bristles fill the width of each letter.

29 | Float the lower two-thirds of each letter with DeLane's Dark Flesh. Begin at the bottom with a side-loaded ½-inch (13mm) angular and walk the float up on each letter.

30 | In the same manner, float the lower third of each letter with Raw Sienna.

31 | Outline each letter with Black Plum. Thin to linework consistency and apply with a no. 0 script liner. Combine Light Mocha + a touch of Mink Tan and use this mixture to paint a fine line just inside the perimeter of each letter.

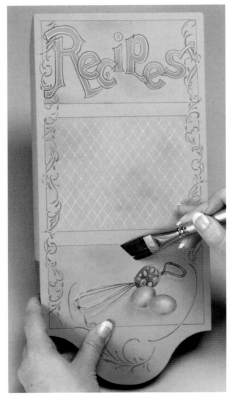

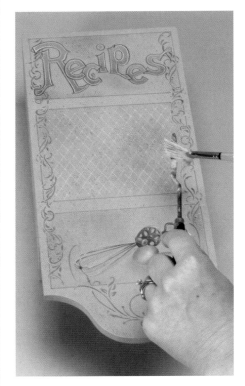

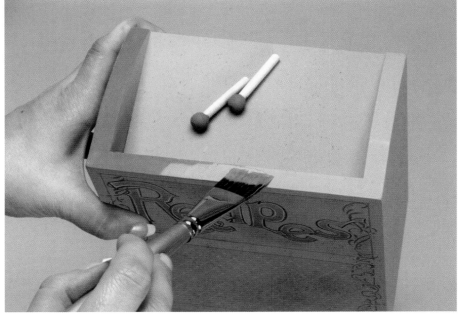

32 WASHES
Using a side-loaded ½-inch (13mm) angular, wash cast shadows of Dried Basil Green + Charcoal Grey (2:1) beneath the eggs and the beater in the bottom panel.

33 Wash subtle patches of color on the three door panels, varying among very thin Dried Basil Green + Charcoal Grey (2:1), Raw Sienna, DeLane's Dark Flesh and Black Plum on a side-loaded ¾-inch (19mm) angular. Because Black Plum is such a dark value, take care to use very thin paint so that it does not become overpowering.

34 SPATTERING
Thin Charcoal Grey with water so that it is transparent and spatter the entire box with a no. 4 stiff bristle fan as explained on page 17. In the same manner, spatter the surface with thin Wisteria.

35 TRIM AND FINISHING
Trim the edges of the door and box with Dried Basil Green + Charcoal Grey (2:1). Paint the ball ends of the dowel pins with the same mixture.

36 Protect the finished painting with multiple layers of varnish. You may want to use an exterior varnish to provide the best protection in a kitchen environment. Let dry and assemble for use.

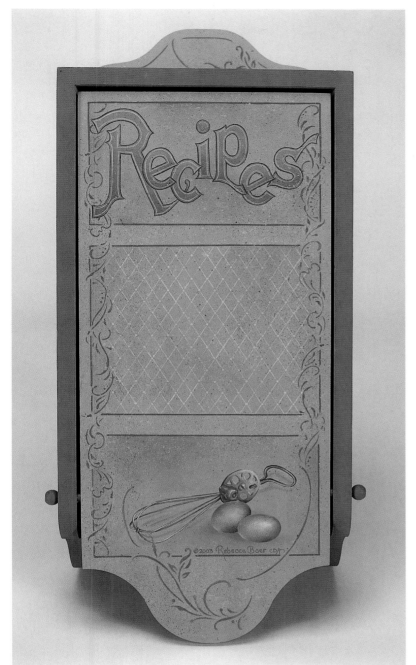

RECIPE BOX: FRONT

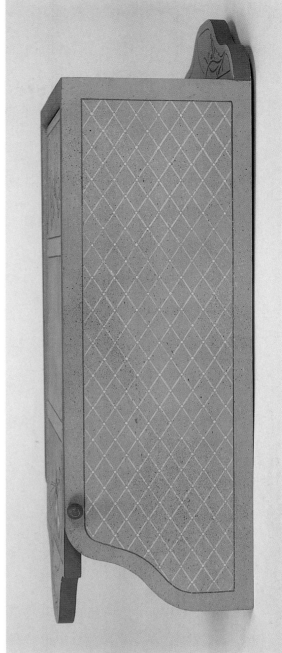

RECIPE BOX: SIDE

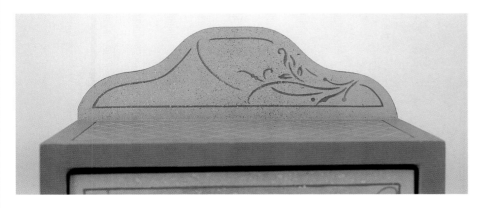

RECIPE BOX: TOP OF FRONT

MAGAZINE BOX
Balancing Lettering With A Descender

This box is the perfect piece for keeping all those magazines neatly in one spot. The simple, yet graceful, berry-and-branch design surrounding the word "Periodicals" will add an elegant touch to any room you choose to put it in. The stenciled design on the sides and back of the box add just enough interest to make this piece a delight to behold from any direction.

colors

PAINT: DecoArt Americana Acrylics

| French Vanilla | Fawn | Dried Basil Green | Marigold | Raw Sienna | Bright Orange | DeLane's Dark Flesh | Rookwood Red | Plum |

| Black Plum | Wisteria | Violet Haze | French Vanilla + Marigold (3:1) | Dried Basil Green + Wisteria (1:1) | Violet Haze + Fawn (5:3) | Violet Haze + Black Plum (1:1) | DeLane's Dark Flesh + Marigold + French Vanilla (1:1:1) | DeLane's Dark Flesh + Rookwood Red (1:1) |

MATERIALS ON THE NEXT PAGE

PATTERN

This pattern may be hand-traced or photocopied for personal use only. Enlarge at 143 percent to bring up to full size.

SURFACE

Magazine box
item 1212 from Wayne's Woodenware

For font identification and help in finding supplies, see Resources on page 126.

BRUSHES

* Mixtique angular, series 8400
  $\frac{1}{8}$-inch (3mm)
  $\frac{3}{8}$-inch (10mm)
  $\frac{3}{4}$-inch (19mm)
* Mixtique round, series 8000, no. 3/0
* Mixtique liner, series 8350, no. 4
* Mixtique script liner, series 8050, no. 0
* American Painter bristle fan, series 2200, no. 4
* Stencil, series 1150, $\frac{3}{4}$-inch (19mm)
* 2-inch (51mm) sponge brush

ADDITIONAL SUPPLIES

* Basic supplies (See page 13.)
* DecoArt Multi-Purpose Sealer
* Fine sanding pad
* Dense foam roller
* Soapstone or chalk pencil
* Cork-backed ruler
* $\frac{1}{4}$-inch (6mm) masking tape
* Loew Cornell Fine Line Painting Pen (optional)
* White transfer paper
* Stencil ST-105 Flourishes & Frills, Simply Elegant Stencils by Rebecca Baer, Inc.
* $\frac{1}{4}$-inch (6mm) graphic tape
* Low-tack tape
* Antibacterial hand gel
* Varnish

1 SURFACE PREPARATION AND BACKGROUND
Trace the pattern but do not transfer at this time. Seal
the box and the insert if desired. When dry, sand lightly
and remove the sanding dust.

Using a dense foam roller, basecoat the front of the
removable insert with Fawn. Do not basecoat the box.
Using a ³/₄-inch (19mm) angular and slightly thinned
Fawn, slip-slap (apply a series of random overlapping
strokes) the color onto the insert. Without rinsing the
brush, proceed to Dried Basil Green + Wisteria (1:1).
Work wet-on-wet, thinning each color slightly as you go.

2 Next, pick up Wisteria. Apply less of this color than
previous colors.

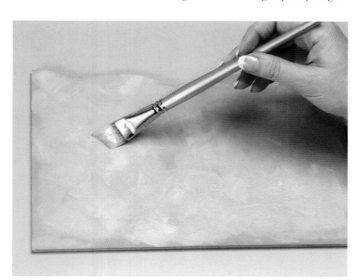

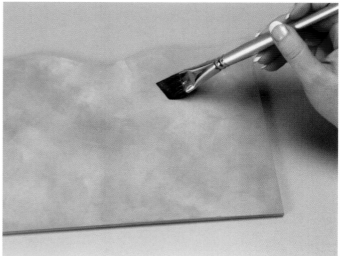

3 Now add a small amount of French Vanilla to the
surface. Apply this color in random patches, taking care
not to overblend. Let dry.

4 Using DeLane's Dark Flesh thinned to wash consistency
and a ³/₄-inch (19mm) angular, scatter a hint of color
randomly over the background. Let dry. In the same
manner, repeat with a hint of Raw Sienna and then
finish with Plum.

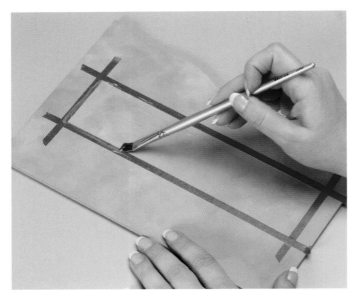

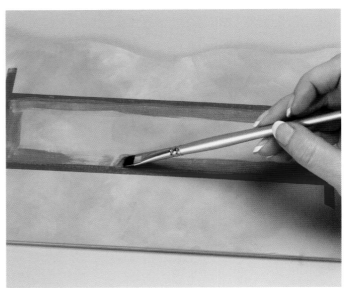

5 | Using a soapstone or chalk pencil and a ruler, refer to your pattern and measure and mark the outer border surrounding the center panel. Tape the perimeter of the border with ¼-inch (6mm) tape, pressing down firmly. Then seal the edges of the tape with a coat of multi-purpose sealer. The sealer may bleed under the tape, but since it will dry clear, this is not a problem. Using the sealer will prevent paint from bleeding beneath the edges of the tape.

6 | Basecoat the border with DeLane's Dark Flesh and a ³⁄₈-inch (10mm) angular. It is helpful to apply the border slightly wider than shown on the pattern to allow for overlap with the center panel. Carefully remove the tape from the surface. It is not necessary for the paint to be dry prior to removing the tape. Measure and mark the boundary for the center panel. Mask the perimeter with tape and seal with multi-purpose sealer. Basecoat the panel with Violet Haze + Fawn (5:3).

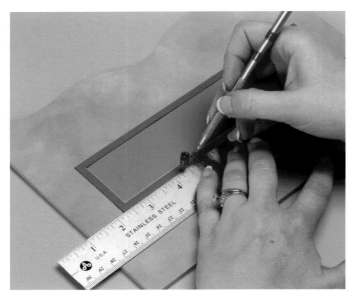

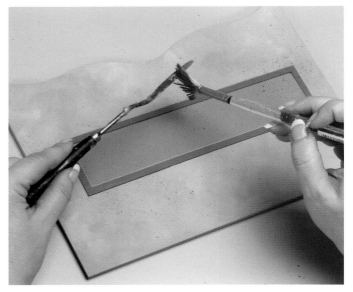

7 | You can trim the border with either a no. 0 script liner or a fine line painting pen. See Recipe Box, steps 6 and 7, page 90, for instructions on the loading and use of the pen. Trim the border along the top and the right sides with a fine line of DeLane's Dark Flesh + Marigold + French Vanilla (1:1:1). Edge the bottom and left sides with Rookwood Red. Clean the painting pen immediately after use to keep the paint from drying and clogging the tip.

8 | Spatter the insert with DeLane's Dark Flesh + Rookwood Red (1:1) and a no. 4 bristle fan, as explained on page 17.

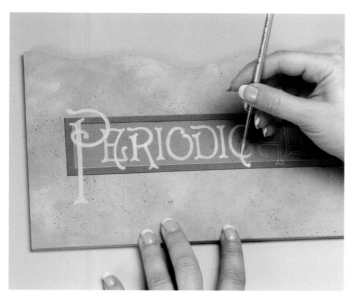

9 | **LETTERING**
Using white transfer paper and your stylus, transfer the lettering portion of the pattern to the panel. Using a no. 4 liner, apply the lettering with French Vanilla + Marigold (3:1).

10 | Shade each letter along the bottom and left with a fine line of Violet Haze + Black Plum (1:1) on a no. 0 script liner.

11 | **BITTERSWEET**
Transfer the remaining pattern. Using a ⅛-inch (3mm) angular, apply a single layer of Delane's Dark Flesh to each berry. Fully opaque coverage is not crucial due to additional layers to be applied over the base.

12 | Daub a small light area in the upper right quadrant of each berry with Bright Orange + a touch of French Vanilla on the tip of a ⅛-inch (3mm) angular. To build the highlight, you will need to pick up additional French Vanilla on the dirty brush and apply it in a small area within the first application so you have a gradual lightening towards the highlight. Increase the proportion of French Vanilla for lighter berries. Daub a tiny highlight of pure French Vanilla on the lightest berries.

13   Float the lower left of each berry with thin Plum on the tip of a ⅛-inch (3mm) angular.

14   With thinned Black Plum on a no. 0 script liner, reinforce the shading with a fine line on the lower left edge of each berry. Using the same brush, daub the blossom end on each berry.

15   Apply the individual petals surrounding the berries with a double-loaded no. 3/0 round. On your palette, combine Raw Sienna + a touch of Black Plum to darken. Load the brush with the Raw Sienna mixture and lightly tip with Marigold. The petals will fill in with only one or two strokes. Allow variety in the double-loaded values to keep all of the petals from looking the same.

16   Daub a tiny highlight of French Vanilla on the petals near the lightest berries. Thin a brush mix of Raw Sienna + a touch of Black Plum to wash consistency. Using a no. 0 script liner, apply in an irregular manner to create branches. In order to develop texture, it is important that the paint is not applied smoothly.

BOX

17 Thin Rookwood Red with water until it is soupy but not transparent. Using a 2-inch (51mm) sponge brush, streak the thinned paint onto the back of the painted panel, being careful to apply the paint with lengthwise strokes in the direction of the wood grain. You may find that the sponge brush skips some areas. The resulting streakiness is desired. It is not necessary to achieve complete coverage.

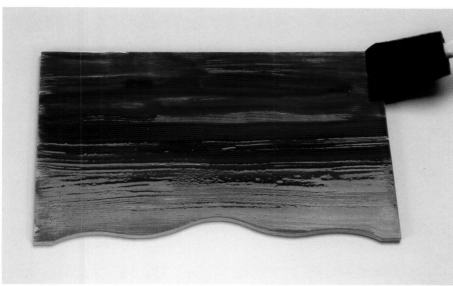

18 Thin Black Plum until it is soupy and apply the thinned paint in the same manner as the Rookwood Red was applied in step 17. Be sure to cover any areas missed during the application of the previous color. When both the Rookwood Red and the Black Plum have been applied, there should be no remaining unpainted areas. There may be some areas that remain translucent, creating a stained appearance, but no raw wood should remain visible. In the same manner, paint all sides of the box, including the edges. Take care to apply the paint in lengthwise strokes in the direction of the wood grain.

19 Basecoat the edges of the removable panel to achieve opaque coverage using Rookwood Red.

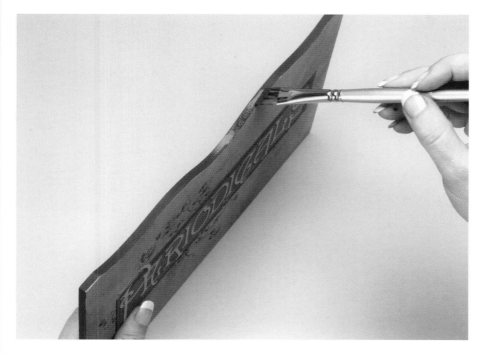

20 STENCILING AND BORDERS

Tape along the perimeter of the exterior box sides as well as the interior and exterior of the box back with ¼-inch (6mm) masking tape, or measure the borders and mark them with a soapstone or chalk pencil. In the same manner, establish a ¼-inch (6mm) border along the top of the painted panel's back. All the stenciling is done with stencil ST-105 Flourishes & Frills. You'll have to reposition the stencil several times, reversing it as needed. To keep the stencil from shifting, secure it with low-tack tape. See the stencil and border positioning photos below to help you determine placement. Pick up Raw Sienna on a ¾-inch (19mm) stencil brush. Wipe the brush on a paper towel to remove excess paint. Holding the brush perpendicular to the surface, pounce over the stencil until the scrollwork is filled in. Due to its intricate detail, the stencil must be cleaned carefully. Refer to the instructions under "Stencil Cleaners" on page 11.

21 Establish a border between the stenciled segments by tracing along the inside of the masking tape with a chalk pencil and then removing the tape. Paint the linework border sections between the stenciled segments with Raw Sienna on a no. 0 script liner. See the stencil and bordering photos below for placement of this linework on the box.

22 Protect all box surfaces with several layers of your favorite varnish.

stencil and border positioning

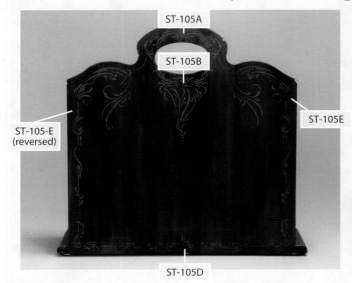

BOX BACK

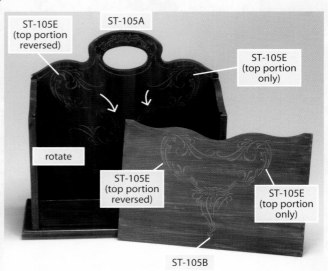

BOX AND INSERT BACK

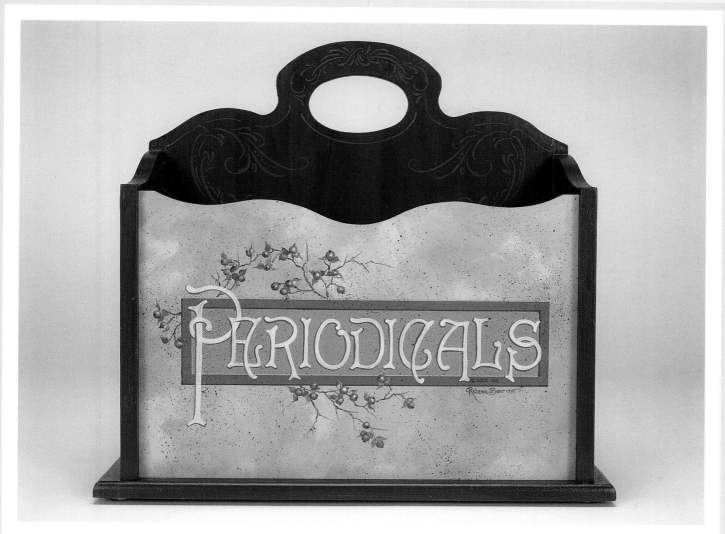

MAGAZINE BOX: FRONT

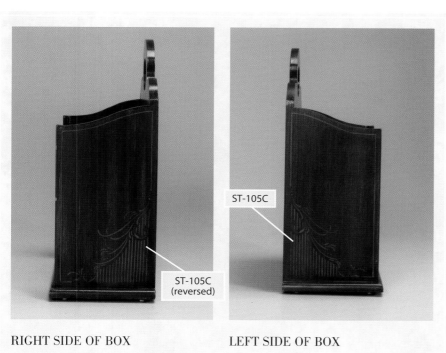

ST-105C

ST-105C
(reversed)

RIGHT SIDE OF BOX   LEFT SIDE OF BOX

ROCKING CHAIR & FOOTSTOOL

Lettering on Fabric

Love Faithfulness Joy Peace Kindness Patience Gentleness

BASED ON THE FRUIT OF THE SPIRIT (GALATIANS 5:22-23)

For these projects, select your fabric first, and you can easily choose paint colors to coordinate. Printed fabric often has a series of color swatches along the selvage edge, which is handy when choosing coordinating colors. Choose a medium-to-dark color for the undercoat and a lighter color for the topcoat.

The fabric covers for the cushions can be as simple or elaborate as you wish. For example, the footstool is covered with a simple, solid-color fabric enhanced with painted lettering, while the seat cushion is more involved, using a center floral panel backed by solid material. If sewing isn't your forté, choose a solid color or subtle print that won't compete with the lettering, and eliminate the rocker's center panel.

colors

PAINT: (DA) = DecoArt Americana Acrylics; (DSS) = DecoArt SoSoft Fabric Paint

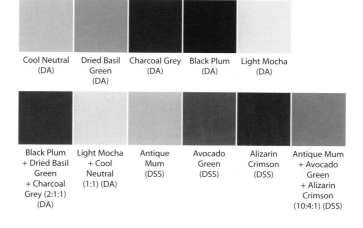

Cool Neutral (DA)	Dried Basil Green (DA)	Charcoal Grey (DA)	Black Plum (DA)	Light Mocha (DA)

Black Plum + Dried Basil Green + Charcoal Grey (2:1:1) (DA)	Light Mocha + Cool Neutral (1:1) (DA)	Antique Mum (DSS)	Avocado Green (DSS)	Alizarin Crimson (DSS)	Antique Mum + Avocado Green + Alizarin Crimson (10:4:1) (DSS)

MATERIALS ON THE NEXT PAGE

SURFACE

Footstool and vintage rocking chair with removable padded seat, available from garage sales, antique stores, home décor retailers

LOEW CORNELL BRUSH

Liner, series 801, no. 6/0

ADDITIONAL SUPPLIES

- Basic supplies (See page 13.)
- Clear Con-Tact paper
- 2 lint-free cloths
- Unscented white candle
- 2-inch (51mm) sponge brush (optional)
- Fine sanding pad
- Varnish (optional)
- Scissors
- Chalk pencil
- Ruler
- Firm panel or Masonite board
- Clear packing tape
- Saral white transfer paper
- Medium-tip ballpoint pen
- Staple gun

FOR CHAIR ONLY

- Fabric equal to the area to be covered plus 12" (30.5cm) on length and width
- Coordinating fabric for center panel (optional)
- Thread to match coordinating fabric
- 1½-inch (3.8cm) thick Poly-fil or foam cushion to fit seat

FOR FOOTSTOOL ONLY

- Fabric equal to the area to be covered plus 12" (30.5cm) on length and width
- 1½-inch (3.8cm) thick Poly-fil or foam cushion to fit footstool
- Fringe for perimeter of footstool
- Decorative brass upholstery tacks (quantity depends on footstool size)
- Hammer

For font identification and help in finding supplies, see Resources on page 126.

Love Faithfulness Joy Peace Kindness Patience Gentleness

PATTERN

This pattern may be hand-traced or photocopied for personal use only. Enlarge at 154 percent to bring up to full size.

SURFACE PREPARATION

1 Because I have no way of knowing what products have been used on vintage pieces prior to my acquisition, I prefer to have any "found" objects dip-stripped and touch-sanded so that I can begin with a fresh surface. Take the surface to a professional refinisher who can dip-strip the surface. This is especially helpful on surfaces with intricate areas where paint and other finishes may be difficult to remove. Alternatively, remove the old finish from the surface, taking care to follow all precautions as directed by the manufacturer of the products that you choose to use.

2 Trace the desired lettering on tracing paper and then cover the tracing with clear Con-Tact paper to prevent tearing. Wash all fabric to remove sizing. Do not use fabric softener. Press, but do not use starch. Remove the padded seat from the rocking chair. If the footstool has a cushion, remove it.

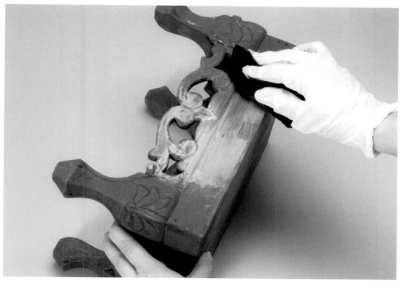

3 PAINTING THE WOOD
The painting procedure is the same for both the rocking chair and the footstool. Combine Black Plum + Dried Basil Green + Charcoal Grey (2:1:1). Using a damp cloth, loosely wipe the color onto the surface. Cover the majority of the surface while allowing random gaps in the coverage.

4 Streak the surface with random patches of wax; any unscented, white candle is suitable. Later, when you sand the top coat, the paint will remove more readily from the waxed areas.

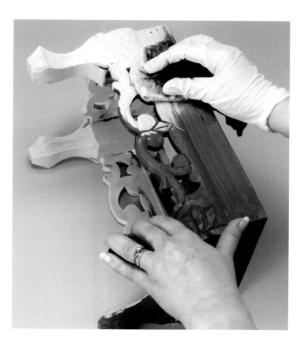

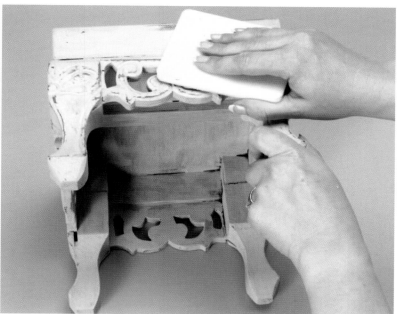

5 Using a damp cloth, wipe on a topcoat of Light Mocha + Cool Neutral (1:1). If you're working on a surface with intricate detail, a sponge brush is helpful to get the paint into small areas.

6 When the topcoat is completely dry, sand the surface with a fine-grit sanding pad. The topcoat should sand away easily where there is wax beneath. You can accelerate the removal of the topcoat by dampening the sanding pad or using an electric palm sander. If you choose to use the damp sanding method or the electric sander, proceed with caution, as the paint will diminish rapidly. The painted surface can remain as is or be protected with a low-sheen finish. Left unfinished, the surface will appear more aged and will continue to wear naturally. Protected with varnish, the surface will maintain the current degree of wear, and any exposed wood will be slightly darker.

7 FABRIC COVERINGS

The photographs on this page show the chair seat fabric, but the instructions also illustrate the procedure for the footstool fabric. Create an outline of the rocking chair seat base and add 4" (10.2cm) to each side. Use this pattern to cut the fabric for the seat cover. In the same manner, allow extra fabric beyond the surface area of the footstool and cut the necessary size fabric. Set the fabric for the footstool cover aside.

Determine the size for the rocking chair seat cover's center panel, add a ⅝-inch (16mm) seam allowance to turn under on each side and cut out the panel fabric. Fold each of the fabric pieces in half to find the center and mark both the vertical and the horizontal centerlines with a chalk pencil and ruler. Using the centerlines on both pieces of fabric as a guide, position the decorative panel on the seat cover fabric and top-stitch it in place by hand or machine.

Use clear packing tape to secure the chair seat fabric to a firm panel, making sure that the area to be painted remains accessible. Pull the fabric tightly to prevent shifting. Use a ruler and a chalk pencil to establish a line 1⅜" (3.5cm) from the center panel on all four sides of the seat fabric. Secure the footstool fabric to a firm panel as directed above and use a ruler and a chalk pencil to establish horizontal lines spaced 2" (5.1cm) apart.

8 Position the bottom of the lettering on the appropriate chalk line and transfer the patterns with Saral white transfer paper and a medium-tip ballpoint pen, which won't snag the pattern as a stylus would. Press firmly to assure clear pattern transfer.

9 Using the no. 6/0 liner, fill in the letters with Antique Mum + Avocado Green + Alizarin Crimson (10:4:1). Apply the paint in the center of each outline and pull the brush over the paint again to spread the coverage and fill in the outline. Allow the painting to dry 48 hours. Remove the fabric from the firm panel and hand wash it gently with mild soap to remove pattern lines. Hang the fabric to dry.

no-sew chair cushion options

- Stencil a center panel using the large lattice panel from stencil ST-106 Lattice & Vines (Simply Elegant Stencils from Rebecca Baer, Inc.).
- Purchase fabric with a panel design printed in the center or choose fabric with a subtle pattern that will not compete with the lettering.

10 ROCKING CHAIR SEAT
ASSEMBLY
Cut the cushion to fit the shape of
the seat base.

11 Trim the corners with scissors to
round the edges.

12 To create a slightly mounded
cushion, place a few Poly-fil
scraps on the seat board under
the Poly-fil cushion.

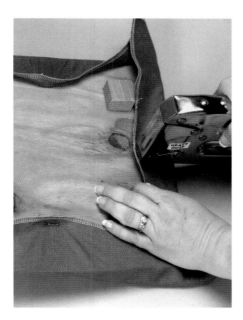

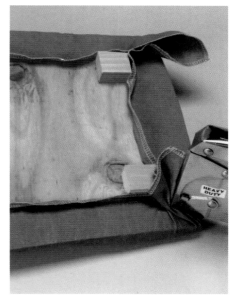

13 Center the completed fabric cover
over the cushion and pull the
excess fabric around to the back.
Pull the fabric taut over the cushion and secure the fabric on the
back of the seat base with a single
staple at the center of each side.

14 Turn the seat over to confirm that
the fabric is still centered before
you continue.

15 Continue to staple the remaining
edges of the fabric, working out
from the center staple and securing
opposite sides to keep the fabric
centered. Pull the corners into
gathers and attach with two to three
staples. Drop the completed cushion in place on the rocking chair.

16 | FOOTSTOOL CUSHION ASSEMBLY
The Poly-fil cushion separates readily and can be adjusted to the desired thickness simply by removing layers. Remove a ½-inch (13mm) layer from the Poly-fil cushion and set it aside for later use.

17 | Cut the remaining Poly-fil to fit the footstool. You can adjust the height by peeling and adding Poly-fil layers.

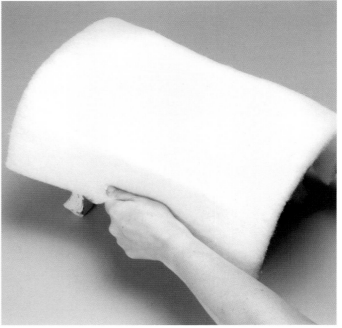

18 | Trim the corners with scissors to round the edges.

19 | Place the ½-inch (13mm) layer of Poly-fil that you set aside previously and pull it firmly over the footstool and Poly-fil cushion to create a smooth surface.

20 | Staple the ½-inch (13mm) layer to the wood sides of the footstool. About one staple every 3 to 4 inches (7.6cm to 10.2cm) is sufficient.

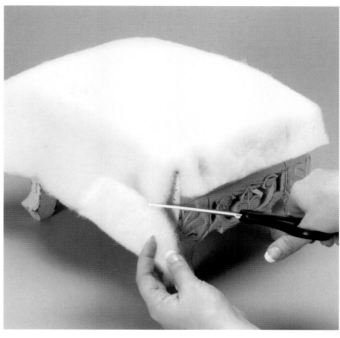

21 | Trim the excess Poly-fil with scissors. To reduce bulk, cut out the corners as shown.

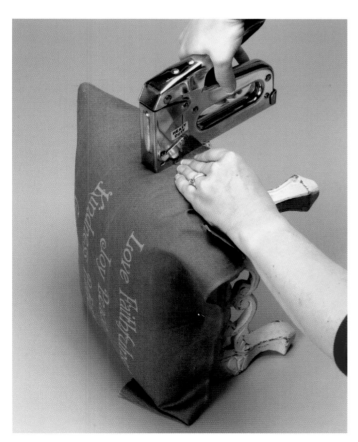

22 | Cover all layers of Poly-fil with the painted fabric, making sure the lettering is centered. Pull the fabric taut and secure the fabric on the stool with a single staple at the center of each side. Confirm that the fabric has remained centered before you continue.

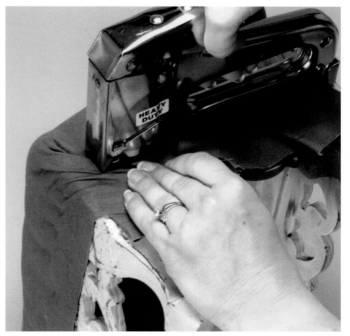

23 | Continue to staple the remaining edges of the fabric, working out from the center staple and securing opposite sides to keep the fabric centered. Gather the fabric at each corner, pull it to the short side of the stool and secure as shown.

24 | Trim away excess fabric so that it will not be seen behind the fringe.

25 | Overlap the edge of one corner on the stool and secure the fringe with one or two staples on each side of the stool. Place your staples vertically so they will be hidden in the grooves of the trim. Fold the end of the trim under before putting in the last staple. If folding the trim end under makes it too thick for the staple, secure with a brass tack.

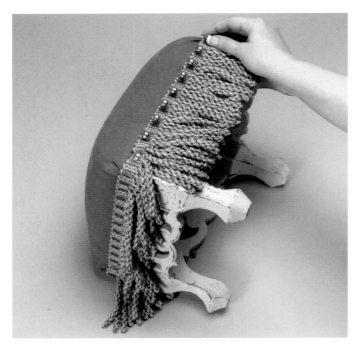

26 | Place the brass tacks lightly in place to establish spacing.

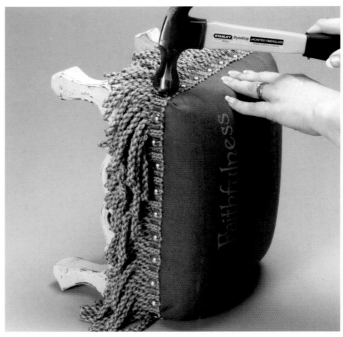

27 | Hammer the tacks in place. If staples show, pull them out right before you hammer the brass tack into that area.

ROCKING CHAIR

ROCKING CHAIR SEAT

FOOTSTOOL

FOOTSTOOL CUSHION

WALL BORDER
Creating a Portable Border

"Friends multiply our joys."

The wall border techniques presented here can be applied directly to your walls if desired. However, I chose to work on polystyrene due to the fact that it has several attractive features. First, polystyrene is easy to work with. It's flexible, requires no preparation, and can be worked on while sitting at a table–which is much more comfortable than standing. Second, it can be easily cut to the desired size or shape with a utility knife. And last, the use of a removable border allows the artwork to be portable without concern about damage. The polystyrene can be removed and re-mounted in a new location. If it does not fit exactly, it can be cut apart and reworked for a different look. Whether painting for yourself or a client, you'll find this versatility a definite plus, given our mobile society and the fact that you need not abandon your beautiful artwork simply because you decide to relocate.

colors

PAINT: DecoArt Americana Acrylics

| Antique White | Driftwood | Raw Umber | Dried Basil Green | Celery Green | Charcoal Grey | Wisteria | Black Plum | Rookwood Red |

| Light Mocha | DeLane's Dark Flesh | Raw Sienna | Dried Basil Green + Wisteria (1:1) | Raw Umber + Dried Basil Green (5:3) | DeLane's Dark Flesh + Rookwood Red (1:1) | Black Plum + Dried Basil Green + Charcoal Grey (2:1:1) | Celery Green + Charcoal Grey + Dried Basil Green (5:3:2) | Dried Basil Green + Raw Sienna (2:1) |

MATERIALS ON THE NEXT PAGE

materials

SURFACE
.30 mil. polystyrene, 9.5" (24.1cm) × any length, available from Milmar Plastics

LOEW-CORNELL BRUSHES
- Mixtique round, series 8000, no. 7
- Mixtique lettering, series 8100
    - $\frac{1}{8}$-inch (3mm)
    - $\frac{1}{2}$-inch (13mm)
- Mixtique script liner, series 8050, no. 0
- Mixtique angular, series 8400, a variety, as needed for leaves
- American Painter fan, series 2200, no. 4

ADDITIONAL SUPPLIES
- Basic supplies (See page 13.)
- Tape measure
- Pencil
- Cutting mat
- Long metal straightedge
- Utility knife
- Dense foam sponge roller
- 3 or more lint-free cloths
- Unscented white candle
- Fine sanding pad
- Water-soluble blue transfer paper (chacopaper)
- DecoArt Multi-Purpose Sealer
- Level
- Soapstone pencil
- Double-faced foam adhesive
- Wood trim
- Finishing nails
- Hammer
- Wood filler
- Paint or stain for trim

For font identification and help in finding supplies, see Resources on page 126.

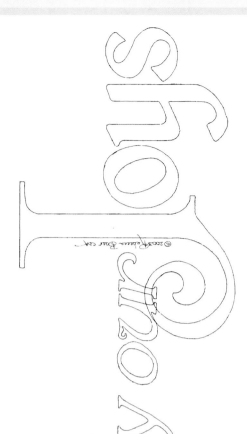

PATTERN
This pattern may be hand-traced or photocopied for personal use only. Enlarge at 125 percent to bring up to full size.

extra quotes

Your lettered wall border can be one repeated quote or a series of quotes. You'll find that the quotes below work well with the quote used in this project.

Kindness *is always in season*

Let Love & Faithfulness *never leave you*

The splendor of beauty is felt in the Heart

PREPARATION

1 Measure the room to determine the length of border material needed. Allow extra for working around windows and doors and for splicing lengths longer than 8' (2.4m). Polystyrene can be purchased in 4' × 8' (1.2m × 2.4m) sheets or ordered pre-cut to a smaller size. If you are using a full sheet, use a tape measure and a pencil to measure, and mark five strips that are each 9.5" (24.1cm) wide and 8' (2.4m) long. At this width, one 4' × 8' (1.2m × 2.4m) sheet will create 40' (12.0m) of border material.

Place a cutting mat or other material under the polystyrene to protect the underlying surface. Cut the strips using a metal straightedge and a utility knife. Do not be concerned with minor irregularities in your cutting. The edges of the border will be covered with trim.

BACKGROUND

2 Using a dense sponge roller, basecoat the surface with Antique White. Using a damp cloth, apply large irregular patches of Dried Basil Green + Wisteria (1:1) to the surface. With a second damp cloth, apply Driftwood in the same manner. Allow some areas with background color to remain visible.

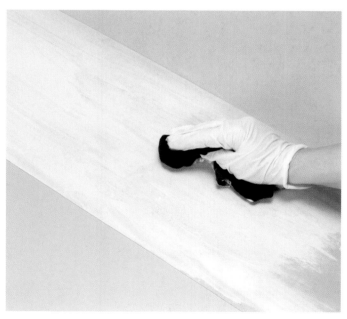

3 Streak the surface with broad, random, lengthwise patches of wax. Any unscented, white candle is suitable.

4 Using a clean, damp cloth, wipe on a topcoat of Light Mocha.

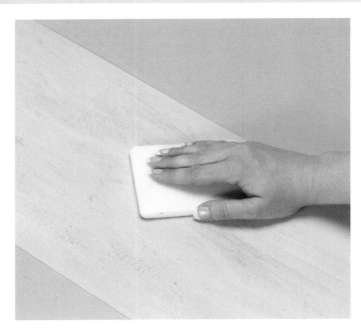

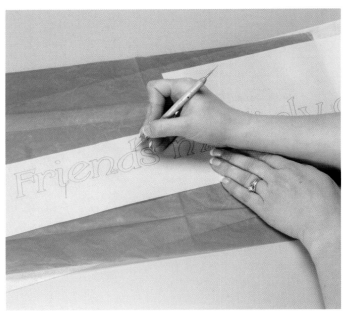

5 | When the topcoat is completely dry, sand the surface with a fine-grit sanding pad. The topcoat should sand away easily where there is wax beneath. You can accelerate the removal of the topcoat by dampening the sanding pad. If you choose to use the damp sanding method, proceed with caution, for the paint will diminish rapidly.

6 | **LETTERING**
Transfer the lettering for your selected phrase(s) using water-soluble blue transfer paper and a stylus.

7 | Paint the large word with thinned Raw Umber + Dried Basil Green (5:3). If the paint beads on the surface, combine the paint with an equal amount of multi-purpose sealer. Because the first letter shown here is done in a flowing, rounded font, I used a no. 7 round to fill it in with shape-following strokes. Complete the remaining letters in this word with the same mixture on a ½-inch (13mm) lettering brush.

8 | Using a ⅛-inch lettering brush, paint the smaller text with DeLane's Dark Flesh + Rookwood Red (1:1).

9 DETAILS
In keeping with the aged appearance, lightly scuff the lettering with a sanding pad.

10 Embellish the border as desired to coordinate with fabric or other features of your décor. It can be as simple or as detailed as you like. I used the color mixes from my palette on page 119 to add leaves and tendrils. These can be done freehand or sketched in before painting. Apply tendrils with a no. 0 script liner.

11 Leaves are applied with a very thin paint on a side-loaded angular. The size of the leaf determines the brush size. Starting at the base of the leaf, float one side, dragging the brush in at random intervals to create texture.

12 Fill the pointed tip with a wedge-shaped float and then texture the opposite side of the leaf.

13   Finish the leaf with a tornado-shaped float along one side of the center vein.

14   Tint and accent the lettering and leaves varying among the colors and mixes from your palette. Thin each application to wash consistency and apply with a ½-inch (13mm) angular.

WALL BORDER

MOUNTING THE BORDER

16 Using a level and a soapstone pencil, draw a line on the wall where the border is desired.

17 Using the level line as a guide, temporarily adhere the border in the desired position using double-faced foam adhesive. This only serves to hold the border in place until permanently secured. Check the lettering with the level to confirm that it is straight.

18 With wood trim cut to the desired length and slightly overlapping the border, nail the trim to the wall, piercing the edge of the polystyrene to hold the border in place. Fill the nail holes with wood filler and, when dry, sand away the excess filler. Paint the trim to coordinate with the room.

15 Using a no. 4 fan, spatter the surface with Black Plum + Dried Basil Green + Charcoal Grey (2:1:1) and then with Light Mocha (see page 17 for spattering instructions).

BORDER TRIM DETAIL

resources

Many of the following items can be found at or ordered through your local decorative painting shop or scrapbooking store. If you don't have a local studio, you'll find many shops now have Web sites from which you can still obtain personalized service and expert advice. Any items not specifically noted here are readily available at any arts and crafts retailer.

General Supplies

brushes, palettes knives & brush basins
LOEW-CORNELL
563 Chestnut Ave.
Teaneck, NJ 07666
www.loewcornell.com
800.922.0186

paints & mediums
DECO ART
P.O. Box 386
Stanford, KY 40484
www.decoart.com
800.367.3047

gray palette paper, Pink Soap & chacopaper
HOUSTON ART, INC.
10770 Moss Ridge Rd.
Houston, TX 77043-1175
www.houstonart.com
800.272.3804

Simply Elegant Stencils
REBECCA BAER INC.
13316 Marsh Pike
Hagerstown, MD 21742-2573
www.rebeccabaer.com
painting@rebeccabaer.com
301.797.1300

J.W. etc.'s Wood Filler, Varnishes & Finishing Wax
J.W. ETC. QUALITY PRODUCTS
2205 First St. #103
Simi Valley, CA 93065
www.jwetc.com

quilter's tape & soapstone pencils
JO-ANN FABRICS
Locate a store near you
www.joann.com
Also available through other sewing retailers.

Ultra Sticky Craft Tape
LÄ DÉ DÄ DESIGNS
14522 Cottage Oak Ave.
Baton Rouge, LA 70810
www.ladeda.com

Etchall Etching Creme, Etchmask, Squeegee & Pick Knife
B&B ETCHING PRODUCTS, INC.
19721 N. 98th Ave.
Peoria, Arizona 85382
www.etchall.com
888.382.4255

Custom Cutting System
CREATIVE MEMORIES
Consultant Kelli Kittel
14542 Barkdoll Rd.
Hagerstown, MD 21742
teachf1161@aol.com
301.824.6626
or locate a consultant near you
through www.creativememories.com

Surfaces

Projects 1 & 2:
PAINTER'S PARADISE
C-10, 950 Ridge Rd.
Claymont, DE 19703-3553
www.paintersparadise.com
jodecart@aol.com
302.798.3897
Fax: 302.478.9441

Project 3
LITTLE'S ANTIQUES & REPRODUCTIONS
102 E. Patrick St.
Frederick, MD 21701
www.littlesfurniture.com
301.620.0517

Projects 4, 5 & 12
MILMAR PLASTICS, INC.
21315 Leitersburg Pike
Hagerstown, MD 21742
www.milmar.com
info@milmar.com
301.739.5730
866.706.1730
Fax: 301.739.8754

Project 6
• CANSON MI-TEINTES
Locate the nearest Canson retailer using the store locator feature on www.canson-us.com
• SCRAPMANIA (for Paper Garden, Creative Imagination and Sanook)
18710 Crestwood Drive
Hagerstown, MD 21742
www.myscrapmania.com
301.393.9111

Project 8
THE CREATIVE C.A.T.
512 Mammouth Rd.
Londonderry, NH 03053
603.437.5947

Projects 9 & 10
WAYNE'S WOODENWARE, INC.
102C Fieldcrest Drive
Neenah, WI 54956
www.wayneswoodenware.com
wayne@wayneswoodenware.com
800.840.1497

Fonts

All fonts used in this book were taken from the books, *100 Ornamental Alphabets* and *Victorian Display Alphabet*, both by Dan X. Solo.
Contact Dover Publications
Customer Care Dept.
31 East Second St.
Mineola, NY 11501-3852
www.doverpublications.com
Fax: 516.742.6953

Project 1: Art Gothic from *100 Ornamental Alphabets*, page 9

Project 2: Carmencita from *100 Ornamental Alphabets*, page 19

Project 3: Anglo from *100 Ornamental Alphabets*, page 7

Project 4: Heather Lightface from *Victorian Display Alphabets*, page 55

Project 5: Houghton from *Victorian Display Alphabets*, page 58

Project 6: Glorietta from *Victorian Display Alphabets*, page 52

Project 7: Wedlock from *Victorian Display Alphabets*, page 99

Project 8: Anglo (modified) from *100 Ornamental Alphabets*, page 7

Project 9: Meistersinger from *100 Ornamental Alphabets*, page 66

Project 10: Eureka from *100 Ornamental Alphabets*, page 43

Project 11: two fonts from *100 Ornamental Alphabets*
• Giraldon Italic, page 54,
• Precosia, page 84

Project 12: three fonts from *100 Ornamental Alphabets*
• Giraldon Italic, page 54,
• Fantasies Estrusques, page 45
• Precosia, page 84

index

The best in decorative painting instruction and inspiration is from North Light Books!

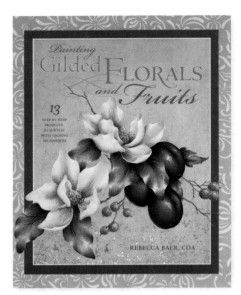

Learn how to enhance your paintings with the classic elegance of decorative gold, silver and variegated accents. Rebecca Baer illustrates detailed gilding techniques with step-by-step photos and invaluable problem-solving advice. Perfect for your home or gift giving, there are 13 exciting projects in all, each one enhanced with lustrous leafing effects.

ISBN 1-58180-261-7, paperback, 144 pages, #32126-K

Stroke by stroke, learn simple lettering techniques for adding words and sayings to all of your projects without the use of patterns or stencils. Bobbie and Jim Gray guide you through the entire alphabet using four easy strokes and show you how to connect the letters into words. You'll achieve professional results in all of your decorative painting with this complete guide.

ISBN 0-89134-961-8, paperback, 128 pages, #31448-K

Overcome the challenge of handlettering with expert advice from Jackie O'Keefe. Featuring over 50 font alphabets to copy or trace, this book offers complete instructions for embellishing, sizing, transferring and painting. You'll find nineteen stroke-by-stroke examples that can be adapted for any decorative painting project.

ISBN 0-89134-825-5, paperback, 128 page, #31202-K

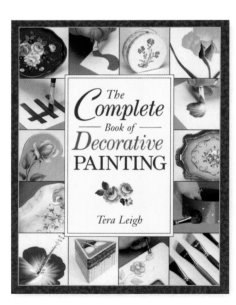

This book is the must-have one-stop reference for decorative painters, crafters, home decorators and do-it-yourselfers. It's packed with solutions to every painting challenge, including surface preparation, lettering, borders, faux finishes, strokework techniques and more! You'll also find five fun-to-paint projects designed to instruct, challenge and entertain you—no matter what your skill level.

ISBN 1-58180-062-2, paperback, 256 pages, #31803-K

These books and other fine North Light titles are available from your local art & craft retailer, bookstore, online supplier or by calling 1-800-448-0915.